British Women's Diaries

AMS STUDIES IN SOCIAL HISTORY, NO. 4
ISSN 0195-8011

Other Titles in This Series:
1. Esmond Wright, ed. *Red, White & True Blue: The Loyalists in the Revolution*, 1976.
2. Richard V. Francaviglia. *The Mormon Landscape.* 1978.
3. Taylor Stoehr. *Free Love in America.* 1979.

British Women's Diaries

A DESCRIPTIVE BIBLIOGRAPHY OF
SELECTED NINETEENTH-CENTURY
WOMEN'S MANUSCRIPT DIARIES

Cynthia Huff

AMS PRESS
NEW YORK

Library of Congress Cataloging in Publication Data

Huff, Cynthia.
  British Women's Diaries.

  (AMS Studies in Social History, ISSN 0195-8011; No. 4)
  Bibliography: p.
  Includes indexes.
  1. Women—Great Britain—History—19th Century—Bibliography.　2. Women—Great Britain—Manuscripts—Bibliography.　3. English Diaries—Women Authors—History and Criticism.　4. English Diaries—19th Century—History and Criticism.　5. English Diaries—Women Authors—Manuscripts—Bibliography.　6. English Diaries—19th Century—Manuscripts—Bibliography.　7. Manuscripts, English—Bibliography.　I. Title.　II. Series.
Z7964.G7H84　1985　　[HQ1593]　　　O16.3054'0941
84-5280　　　　　　　　　　　　　　　ISBN 0-404-61604-6

COPYRIGHT © 1985 BY AMS PRESS, INC.
All rights reserved.

Manufactured in the United States of America

Table of Contents

ACKNOWLEDGMENTS	vii
INTRODUCTION	ix
BRITISH WOMEN'S DIARIES: A DESCRIPTIVE BIBLIOGRAPHY OF SELECTED NINETEENTH-CENTURY WOMEN'S MANUSCRIPT DIARIES	
Aristocracy	1
Gentry	29
Professional-Commercial	41
Intelligentsia	79
Religious	89
INDEX OF DIARISTS	121
SUBJECT INDEX	124

ACKNOWLEDGMENTS

I would like to thank all those who have supported and encouraged my interest in women's diaries. Florence Boos deserves particular appreciation for enthusiastically fostering my original fascination with diaries and equally importantly, for suggesting that I publish my research. She has been an indefatigable reader whose perceptive suggestions have made this book more useful and interesting. I am also indebted to Joel Haefner for his extensive commentary and sympathetic insights and for typing the manuscript. I am grateful to Adelaide Morris for her painstaking yet sensitive reading of the manuscript, to W. R. Irwin for his probing questions about aspects of the diary, to Wendy Deutelbaum for her insightful connections between the diary and the family, to Fred McDowell for his vast knowledge of Victorian culture, and to Alan Long for his exacting remarks about the introduction. My parents, William and Mary K. Huff, deserve special gratitude for their long years of loving support. I am also grateful to my best friend Amy for providing caring companionship and for urging me to continue writing.

The entire project could not have been realized without a Fulbright Research Grant which enabled me to read the primary material which composes this bibliography. For the privilege of that experience I am indebted to the Fulbright Commission and to J. O. A. Herrington. Finally, I would like to thank the archivists of the Friends' Society Library; the Gloucestershire Record Office; the Hertfordshire Record Office; the National Library of Scotland; the National Library of Wales; University College Library; and the Wigan Record Office for their help and interest in locating the appropriate material.

INTRODUCTION

Not long after the close of the nineteenth century, Virginia Woolf speculated about the form and content of diaries while writing her own. Characteristically, she decided that she would like hers "to resemble some deep old desk, or capacious hold-all, in which one flings a mass of odds and ends." Yet she realized too that the diary could not be shapeless, for "looseness quickly becomes slovenly," and she feared her own diary writing "becoming slack and untidy."[1] Woolf's comments in many ways capture the impulse and practice of diary writing for nineteenth-century British women. Women in the last century wrote diaries because they wished to embrace the flux of life, to store its nuances in a place of safe keeping, so that when the time came they could sift and evaluate the past, whether it was measured by the recurrence of birth and death or by the tallying of accounts. As Woolf realized, creating a diary is a skill which requires the manipulation of the vastness of experience. By deciding what to enter in her diary and which form to use to encase the record of her life, each of the diarists represented in this bibliography tells her own story in her own way.

Recently scholars have recognized our need to hear the stories told by little-known or neglected women, for only by hearing their voices can we rightfully evaluate our own past and their place within it. Echoing Virginia Woolf, Elaine Showalter emphasizes that the extraordinary woman must be viewed in relation to her contemporaries, and, furthermore, that the study of women's lives provides new pathways for the investigation of numerous other disciplines.[2] Her comments are generally confirmed by scholars of women's studies, who are keenly aware of the necessity for uncovering the writings of women, not only because these are fascinating accounts, but also because these records contain much information about medical practices, the configuration of the family, recreational activities, child care, political events, and social customs.[3] This bibliography should be seen as another tool to help reconstruct the lives of ordinary women and to aid in the pursuit of interdisciplinary, historical, and literary studies.

I conceived this bibliography as a descriptive and analytical work, because of my own frustration with brief listings of source material, and because friends and colleagues also found the starkness of truncated references annoying. I am deeply indebted to William Matthews, whose extensive bibliography of <u>British Diaries: 1442-1942</u> (Los Angeles: University of California Press, 1950) brought the existence of numerous diaries

INTRODUCTION

to scholarly recognition, and to John Stuart Batts, whose British Manuscript Diaries of the Nineteenth Century (Totowa, N.J.: Rowman and Littlefield, 1976) provided the impetus for my own research. Like Matthews and Batts, I list manuscripts chronologically by their earliest date of composition.

However, my departure from their methods is significant. While their entries are relatively brief, mine are more extensive, since I wish to emphasize all the major elements in a diarist's life and indicate the important configurations within it. Hence this bibliography is interpretive as well as informational. Further, to provide an additional category of reference, I also arrange the diarists according to their social class--whether upper or middle--and subdivide these designations according to the occupation of the head of the household. Hence, the upper-class diarists are subdivided into members of the aristocracy and of the gentry, while middle-class diarists encompass three groups: the professional-commercial, the intelligentsia, and the religious. Each subdivision is designated by a letter: "A" designates aristocracy; "G" gentry; "PC" professional-commercial; "R" religious; and "I" intelligentsia. Within each social group the diaries are numbered consecutively according to their earliest date of composition. Thus, the diary of Jane Johnston, begun in 1817, is designated "PC4", the fourth earliest professional-commercial diary, while the fifth earliest journal in this social group, that of Eliza Hope Stevens, is listed "PC5". This allows the reader not only to identify quickly the social classification of each diarist, but also to locate through the subject index the social groups whose members wrote most often about a given topic.

These social classifications were derived mostly from internal evidence in the diaries, supplemented by whatever external information could be uncovered. Because the women whose diaries are listed in this bibliography are little-known, in many cases it is extremely difficult to find much supplementary biographical information. That, however, makes it all the more imperative that the contents of their diaries be brought to light, since these documents help fill gaps in our knowledge of women and their lives in the last century.

The women represented here come from the upper and middle classes, although a few diarists belong to skilled artisans, a group located on the boundary between the middle and working classes. I was unable to find examples of working class diaries, perhaps because these women seldom had the opportunity or education to keep a diary, or because their diaries have not been preserved. I included that small class of diarists labeled intelligentsia because of their extensive impact upon the intellectual life of the nation. The division labeled religious comprises both diaries of clergymen's families and journals kept by women for spiritual purposes; while women who were related to clergymen did not necessarily

INTRODUCTION

write spiritual diaries, such an amalgamation nonetheless usefully separates these diarists from their contemporaries. The largest number of diarists belong in the category of professional-commercial, partly because this designation encompasses so many diverse occupations, a number of which were just emerging in the nineteenth century.

The diarists I have selected come from many parts of Great Britain and the colonies, and their diaries cover the span of the century, and include records composed by women at each point in their lives between girlhood and death. The manuscripts of the diaries are housed in easily-accessible repositories such as national libraries and public record offices.

Not only the choice of the diaries, but also the composition of this bibliography is designed with multiple purposes in mind. Each of the entry divisions of format, content, and stylistic features forms an integral yet distinct part of the whole diary. Entries in previous bibliographies have tended to be little more than brief listings of the work's contents, with no consideration of the make-up of the volume itself. Like other works of literature, diaries differ in their arrangement, and by studying this we can determine much about the diary and its writer. When there is more than one volume, I have listed the number extant.

Nineteenth-century British women's manuscript diaries are of two types: those kept in a printed format and those whose format is self-determined. The self-determined volumes are usually bound, although in a few cases the diary keeping impulse exerts so much influence that the writer creates a makeshift journal of single sheets of paper folded together. In the self-determined diary the writer is free to choose the format, which can vary from daily to yearly entries and may include newspaper clippings, sketches, and poems, as well as notations of expenditures or addresses. The printed format is imposed on the diarist, although the writer often ignores and violates the rules, spaces, dates, and arrangements dictated by the diary publishers.

One of the primary features of diaries with printed formats is their compendium of useful information, since they were intended by their publishers to function simultaneously as personal records, almanacs, and account books. The blurring of the distinctions between the monetary and the personal, as well as between the public and the private, is especially strong in volumes with printed formats, where the diarist enters her comments alongside pages for accounts. Such an ordering facilitates an equation of monetary reckoning and personal evaluation. Furthermore, the inclusion in diaries with printed formats of certain types of public information and features of popular entertainment provide a direction and framework for the diarist's rendition of her life.

The contents of diaries with printed formats changed

over the course of the century. As entertainment began increasingly to center on the acquisition of goods, the rebusses, charades, and Vauxhall songs which were common in the first few decades gave way to a spate of advertisements at the close of the Victorian era. Such a change betokens the different attitudes at the beginning and the end of the nineteenth century, and indicates as well how the study of diaries with printed formats can help the social historian determine trends.

Analyzing the format of these diaries helps determine the writer's self-conception and social class, since the majority of the printed volumes cited in this bibliography were specifically designed for ladies. By selecting a volume entitled a "Ladies' Diary," a writer provides a possible clue to her class, and certainly to her self-image, while the printed contents of such volumes indicate what the general interests of ladies were supposed to be. The publishers of these diaries felt their buying public would be entertained by color fold-outs, especially common at the beginning of the century, but they also thought information would attract their audience. In accord with Virginia Woolf's idea of the diary as a catch-all, printed diaries list facts about virtually everything from foreign postage to taxes on lunatics. Interestingly, many of the advertisements in printed volumes feature other diaries.

In addition to the printed contents of diaries, the writer's use of such a volume is significant. The spaces for the diarist's comments in volumes with printed formats are ordinarily quite restricted, and the majority of the writers reacted to this by spilling their remarks into the spaces designated for other entries or by continuing certain entries at the back of the volume. Occasionally diarists failed to compose entries in the spaces allotted to a particular day, and in such instances the writer merely redated the entries. A lack of spacing between entries or comments entered both vertically and horizontally are common in some self-determined volumes.

Yet another feature common to both self-determined diaries and diaries with printed formats is the summary and anniversary entry. The memoranda space in many diaries with printed formats is meant to function as an ordering device, an opportunity for the diarist to review her actions, but frequently the space is not used by the writer for this purpose. Instead, diarists write summary and anniversary entries when noteworthy or recurrent events take place. Childbearing, family deaths, birthdays, wedding anniversaries, and the end of the year serve as pauses in the diarist's life and occasions for composing retrospective entries. Entries which merely summarize a period of time during which the writer has been unable to compose her diary usually occur after childbirth or a family death. In such cases the diarist primarily recounts the event. However, the purpose of entries written on anniversaries is usually self-evaluation and reflection, for here the diarist considers the past year's texture and activities as well as her recent behavior, and looks forward to the coming year.

If diaries were merely composed diurnally they might be the untidy creations which Virginia Woolf feared, but instead their narrative structure shows recurrent traits which provide them with a discernible form. Rather, diaries are structured by significant events in the writer's life whose occurrence must be considered when determining the arrangement of the individual diary and the perimeters of the genre. Anniversary and summary entries serve an important function in the diary's arrangement, since they act as divisions which are roughly analogous to chapters in a novel or stanzas in a poem.

These nineteenth-century manuscript diaries also exhibit common stylistic properties, and in the bibliography the entry division entitled "Stylistic Features" attempts to point out some of these. Diaries have often been considered highly personal, almost solipsistic, compositions whose secretive quality is symbolized by a lock. However, such a conception of the diary is at odds with the stylistic features of nineteenth-century manuscripts, where the use of the first person plural pronoun indicates that diaries were often written as family documents. Diarists frequently employ "we" rather than "I," and their common omission of the singular pronoun makes their entries seem distanced rather than intimate. The collective quality captured by the use of "we" points to a society where the family rather than the individual was often the most important unit, and where women in particular were expected to subsume their identity in the familial configuration. "We" is also employed by diarists when they are composing their works as travelogues where its use again shows its collective function.

A reading of nineteenth-century manuscripts indicates the self-reflexive qualities of the genre. Many diarists appear to be aware of an audience, for they often begin their journals by addressing a possible future reader, often themselves at some later date, or a family member. Because a woman was frequently the designated chronicler of family records, she copied out the diaries of family members, but she might also render another's diary because of its importance for herself. One way of learning about the thoughts and activities of a friend or relative was to read her diary or to hear it read aloud. The well-established practice of diary reading may help account for the frequent use of "we," since this is a narrative device which includes the reader or listener and which, consequently, was often used by nineteenth-century novelists.[4]

Yet other stylistic features point to the conscious craft of diary writing and indicate that Virginia Woolf's sense of the diary as both a carefully considered product and a catch-all captures its seemingly contradictory essence. Diarists apparently often reread their journals and edited them, since additional comments and crossed-through words and phrases appear in the manuscripts. These changes indicate the writer's awareness of an audience just as their tendency to use circumlocutions does. When the diarists considered a word or phrase objectionable, they wrote in a foreign language or employed dots and dashes. Their inclination to mark over pencilled entries with ink also indicates the diarists' sense of their creations as something permanent.

Diarists' habitual use of standard narrative techniques helps give their writing a literary tone and quality. In many diaries the writer narrates one or more deathbed scenes, and to capture the drama of the moment, uses quotation marks throughout the dialogue. Long narrative accounts of important events or conversations are a staple in many journals. Diarists often relate anecdotes with a novelistic verve, providing punchlines, moral plots, character delineations, and well-constructed scenes.

The tone and intent of diaries can change rapidly from humorous to solemn, as the author switches from narrating a fascinating incident to addressing God. The direct addresses to the Lord, which occur most commonly in summary and anniversary entries, seem closely related to the sermons and prayers which were a daily ingredient in the lives of nineteenth-century women. In addition to addressing God about spiritual matters, diarists also sought His help during dire circumstances such as childbirth, illness, or death. In such instances their sentence length and structure usually varies from its normal pattern. The change in the structure and length of sentences often signals a shift in import in the diaries, just as it does in other kinds of narrative. Diarists who write more about their inner lives tend to write longer sentences and entries, while the women who concentrate on outside events construct more fragments and shorter entries. The latter may occur partly because so many fragmentary phrases and terse entries are frequently extensions of account books.

The content of nineteenth-century British women's manuscripts is as wide-ranging as the concept of the diary as a "capacious hold-all" would imply. At one end of the spectrum of possible journal forms stands the account book. Some of the manuscripts included in this bibliography are primarily account books, though women often combined the rendering of accounts with comments about their daily lives or their spiritual progress. The variety of items listed in even a short volume employed for keeping accounts is staggering; and this type of diary indicates the complexity and diversity of nineteenth-century life as well as the numerous discrepancies between it and our own. The cost of hair oil, chimney pots, and mahogany screens, as well as of staple items such as coal, beer, and sugar commonly appear in diaries, which are an excellent source for the expenditures of everyday life in the last century. Naturally, the items or expenses which occur in diaries changed somewhat over the course of the century. It is common in diaries written during the first few decades of the nineteenth century to see listings of amounts won or lost at cards, while later diarists include the cost of train travel. Women also frequently record the cost of hiring servants and laborers.

The extensive keeping of accounts in diaries shows the scope of women's managerial functions and business acumen. Since women frequently employed their diaries to keep track of the estate's affairs, they were often responsible for recording variables such as weather changes, harvest yields, and the acquisition of animals. In fact, comments about the weather form such a regular feature in the diaries that they are not noted in the index.

Another type of diary represented in the bibliography is the travel journal. Often, the travelogue forms only a part of the diarists' record, since many simply used the same volume to record their activities at home and during their journeys. At home or traveling, the diarists commonly noted who visited or dined, and what entertainments they attended, but there are some features unique to the travel journal. Travel narratives frequently include sketches and postcards, and the more interesting accounts reveal the writer's attitude toward foreigners. On the whole the British diarists were quite xenophobic, and contrast unfavorably the customs of others with their own. The elasticity of the diary form permits the capturing of diverse experiences and the molding of opinion, both concomitants of travel. Diarists often wrote accounts of their sojourns for the enjoyment and information of family and friends as well as for their own recollection; and when their diaries assume the configuration of travelogues they become similar to the accounts of tours so popular during the Victorian era and one of the forerunners of modern travel brochures.

Since they primarily record things, whether expenditures or daily activities, both travel journals and account books are outer-directed diaries. Outer-directed diaries concentrate not so much on the writer's reactions to events, but on the events themselves, and the diarist's comments about physical possessions are ordinarily rendered without any indication of how these relate to her life. Outer-directed diaries focus on the accoutrements of the writer, whether her collection of objects takes the form of places visited or the acquisition of goods. The outer-directed diary accords with Woolf's definition of the form as a "capacious hold-all," for it places side-by-side "a mass of odds and ends," without necessarily indicating their relationship to one another or to the diarist.

If travelogues and account books stand at one end of the spectrum of diary forms, the religious record, which presents inner rather than outer experience, stands at the other. Like account books and travelogues, the religious diary is constructed with a definite purpose. Even though the religious impulse may not dominate the entire diary, writers often become more spiritually inclined after the occurrence of momentous events. Nineteenth-century British women frequently set out to compose diaries whose primary intent was to evaluate their spiritual progress and to cite their participation in religious observances and activities. The Quakers in particular wrote diaries which record their attendance at monthly meetings, visits to the faithful and to possible converts, and spiritual tribulations and triumphs. Since important religious activities are repeated at specified times and the Quakers' experiences are related to their religious and social commitment, much of the content of their journals is relatively predictable.

Other religious diarists tend to follow similar patterns. Intensely spiritual diarists tend to see God's hand everywhere, and to view others as exemplars. Most diarists consider some relatives or friends as exemplary; and, especially when a loved one has died, she may eulogize the noble characteristics of this individual. In their zeal to improve their behavior and become more worthy Christians, religious diarists consistently compare themselves, usually to their disparagement, to some worthy individual. The esteemed person is often the diarist's minister, but it can also be

Christ, a Biblical character, or a dying person.

Especially if they had suffered intensely and patiently, the dying were considered particularly saintly. One of the major activities of religious diarists is visiting the terminally ill. Since this was a form of charity considered appropriate to the female domain and sensibilities, providing solace to the dying was not restricted to any one group of women. But those who were religious were especially committed to this pursuit. Their records are filled with deathbed scenes which emphasize the beauty of death and its release from worldly trials into perpetual bliss. Religious diarists narrated deathbed scenes for much the same reason that they held up others as exemplars: in both cases the diarists wished to alter their own behavior to accord with spiritual teachings.

Diaries kept by very religious women are geared toward altering the self and relating personal experience; like other inner-directed diaries, they tend to be structured around personally significant events. Anniversaries serve as milestones which afford the diarist an opportunity to review her past, to anticipate the future, and to evaluate her behavior. Yearly anniversaries necessitate a periodic review of the diarist's self, which underscores and accentuates the journal's purpose of shaping behavior.

Religious diaries are not the only type of personal record designed to effect moral reformation. Nineteenth-

Introduction

century British children were encouraged by their parents to write diaries, and journals were given as gifts to both children and servants. It is common to read in manuscript diaries that a young child is told to keep an account of his or her life so that he or she can recall past actions and hence learn to correct mistakes and use time wisely.

Perhaps the extreme example of the diary's use in molding the behavior of children occurs when a governess details her pupil's progress. Since the teacher not only records the ratings achieved in various subjects by the student, but also comments obliquely on her relationship with her pupil and employer, behavior book diaries reveal as much about the governess as about the pupil. Although behavior books may have an ostensibly objective purpose in mind, they imply much about the governess's social position, and her educational expectations and beliefs. They serve as excellent source material about the role of the governess in the last century; and their rhetorical construction is complex enough to reward students fascinated by this unusual autobiographical form.

For many women, the diaristic impulse is less directed than account books or religious records. The journals composed by nineteenth-century women tend instead to amalgamate the qualities of inner- and outer-directed diaries. Entries vary from sketchy listings to long, personally revealing descriptions of important events. Such diaries are a good source for an examination of the genre's form and content, as they include a wide spectrum of topics, styles, and structures. Areas of interest and common configurations recur in the diary, and certain events ordinarily experienced by nineteenth-century women provide the key to both the form and content of most manuscript journals. A woman's depiction of her life varies, of course, depending on her age and the years in which she wrote. Younger women are more preoccupied with marriage while older women focus on death. Given such variables, the diaries include comments about marriage and men, service and self-identity, public events and family experiences.

Children may begin writing about their lives because their parents urge it, but even diaries which are initiated through a sense of duty usually only continue if they help the writer evaluate her life. The diary allows its creator to sift and mold her existence, and the very act of writing gave nineteenth-century women a sense of control and identity they might otherwise have lacked. Keeping a diary enabled women to enter their achievements and failures, sort out their relationships, and converse with an understanding friend, a role the diary often filled. Although these processes are intrinsic to the very act of composing a diary, they are most prevalent in the accounts maintained by girls and young women.

Two topics which surface again and again in diaires

written early in life are marriage and the desire to be male. In the last century girls were painfully aware both of the inferior status of their sex, and of men's inability to live up to their exalted position. Young women commonly imagined what they would do had they been born male, for many desired to make their mark in the world. The accident of birth prevented them from pursuing many of their goals, because women's social and political power was limited in the last century. Young women most resented their lack of freedom. Some fantasized about being missionaries in India to convert unbelievers, but many, attracted by pomp and glory, wished to become soldiers, and virtually all desired the escape from confinement which they felt males enjoyed. Young women in the nineteenth century, of course, saw their brothers reap the benefits of an education far superior to their own, and experienced as well the restrictions of chaperonage.

Accompanying women's expression of their wish for greater influence was a gnawing sense that men's superior status was largely a social construction. Men and the relationship between the sexes are frequent subjects in nineteenth-century women's diaries, though some modern readers may be startled that such topics were discussed not only by radical feminists but by ordinary women as well. Despite some acceptance of stereotypes of female purity and passivity and male worldliness and aggressiveness, the diarists saw men as considerably more flawed than the ideal of the omniscient, benevolent patriarch would suggest. One diarist commented that men failed to see the humanity of the Indian servants they despised, while another expressed her disdain for the opposite sex by writing "men" in miniscule letters. Though aware that men were supposed to possess superior attributes, she commented that all the ones she knew were mean and ignoble. Even though young women tended to criticize men in general, they often made exceptions for brothers and husbands.

The relationship between brothers and sisters in the last century was complex, and further study might help unravel the intricacies of nineteenth-century family structures. Because males had a superior education and greater physical freedom, sisters often had to rely on their brothers for knowledge. Too, the closeness of siblings encouraged a sense of companionship between sisters and brothers, and throughout their lives women frequently asked their brothers for assistance rather than their husbands. Circumstances would encourage a young woman to consider her brothers, especially the eldest, as more exemplary than other males. The eldest brother frequently achieved this position by tutoring his sisters. Some diaries detail these methods of instruction as well as the diarist's desire to adhere to the moral code her oldest brother exemplified. There are instances where a sister's adoration of an elder brother resembles her love of Christ; her diary is a monument to his achievements.

But their diaries serve too as a means of enabling women to cope with marriage, a momentous change which frequently symbolized loss and death. Young women dreaded marriage because it meant leaving the family home and the security of close and long-established relationships and a familiar milieu. Many agonized about the advent of marriage and came to accept betrothal only by exalting the superior qualities of the husband, who to some extent psychologically replaced the eldest brother. Most young women knew their husbands merely cursorily before they married, and many congratulate themselves if during the new couple's honeymoon they socially act like brother and sister.

Marriage structures nineteenth-century British women's manuscript diaries. The diarists' detailed descriptions and their recognition of their altered position indicates the importance of the wedding day. Entries depicting the day of the wedding are quite long, and note the guests at the wedding breakfast and service, the exact time and place of the ceremony, her behavior throughout, and, most significantly, her new status as wife. The diarists express their awareness of their new identity by referring to their husbands by their Christian names for the first time.

In the last century childbirth usually closely followed marriage. Parturition served as another important chapter in many diarists' lives and enabled women to shape their accounts. Childbirth constituted a journey into fear and anxiety for nineteenth-century women, as the dangers of disease and death were great. Understandably, Victorian women did not distinguish between childbirth and other bodily disorders; and given the fact that women had ample reason to fear for their lives, it is not surprising that they used their diaries to prepare themselves for the momentous event and to record their symptoms. Two sisters, who were both expecting their first child, passed a series of secret notes back and forth. This practice, which is recorded in one sister's diary, must have mitigated the anguish and pain of pregnancy by helping to establish and maintain female solidarity. Since diaries were commonly read by female friends and relatives, the similarities in the way pregnant women constructed their entries may point to an existing ritual bond among women.

The account of the birth itself is especially significant, for this is virtually always a summary entry which provides an important pause in the diary and the diarist's life, and, like the descriptions of marriage, follows a pattern. Although the entry detailing the birth may be written several months later, the mother is very scrupulous about noting when she was taken ill, who attended the confinement, the precise time of the birth, and her reactions to it. Yet another common feature of the entries about parturition is the expression of fear and anxiety, and to avoid further alarming family members, mothers often confided their distress to their diaries.

Introduction

When not engaged in the process of childbearing, nineteenth-century women often nursed the sick and assisted other women during childbirth. Since diaries were used to record these activities, they serve now, as they did then, as compendia of details about parturition and disease. Many accounts become primarily descriptions of the illnesses undergone by friends and relatives. They serve other purposes too. Because diaries were commonly read by others, they were apparently a source for much medical information and helped women reinforce their prescribed roles as nurses. Diaries also enabled women to mold themselves according to the community's expectations and to play their proper part in the support system provided by women during childbirth. Ironically, nineteenth-century women's ability to use their diaries to cope with the ordeals of disease and childbirth may have hindered us from properly judging their social contributions. Contrary to popular belief, Victorian women were not idle or mere trophies exhibited by their husbands, for the large role disease played in their lives, either through childbirth or nursing, forced them continually to employ their time usefully.

Women in the last century were not always involved in nursing or childbirth. Manuscript diaries indicate that women participated in the public life of Britain, even though they did so less than men. Because women could not vote, their interest in politics was largely vicarious. Some diarists followed political developments closely, especially if a relative were active in Parliament, and virtually all noted particularly newsworthy events in the government. The condemnation of Napoleon is a common strain in diaries written early in the century, as are comments about social unrest, which indicate class bias.

Women's perception of the significant cultural events and activities which helped mold nineteenth-century society provides a more complete portrait of the age. Diaries written in the middle years of the century contain descriptions of and reactions to the Great Exhibition and the coming of the railroad. Then as now, London epitomized Britain, and whether a diarist called it her home or was merely a sojourner, she recorded London plays and exhibitions, sights, such as the British Museum or the Bank, and lectures, public readings, and religious services. The last were not activities confined to London since all are staples in nineteenth-century manuscript diaries. Remarks about reading and sports are also prevalent. Riding horseback was common for women throughout the century, while towards the end croquet and tennis came into vogue. Many diaries contain lengthy lists of the writer's reading, and often women used their accounts to respond to character delineation, especially of women.

Although women were certainly a part of male cultural and recreational activities, their role and their identity centered on serving others. Entertainment and educational endeavors often fell under the rubric of service, since women escorted children to enlightening and amusing events or supervised these at home. But clearer expressions of service were performing secretarial duties, dispensing charity, and nursing the sick and dying. Diaries may function partly as account books because wives and unmarried daughters often acted as secretaries for the head of the household, though occasionally a young woman would perform these duties for her mother. Consequently, manuscript diaries contain notations of letters written, bills paid, and household items procured. The diaries also show women's participation in an extensive system of charity, for they describe distributing coal and blankets to the poor, giving money to the needy, and teaching and supervising in schools for destitute children.

As the professions began to assume their twentieth-century configuration and as more of the functions of service were taken over by the state, the diversity of duties engaged in by women started to diminish. This trend may have accounted in part for the inaccurate contemporary view of nineteenth-century women as useless. However, as their diaries attest, the life of women revolved around the duties of service. Writing and re-reading their diaries must have made women conscious of their identity through the rendering of service and confident about their place in nineteenth-century society.

Because much of a woman's life was spent nursing the

sick and dying, deaths and illnesses form a large portion of nineteenth-century manuscript diaries. Writers often used their journals to cope with the loss occasioned by the demise of friends and relatives. Older women, in particular, concentrated on the loss of loved ones, and their diaries seem to have helped them prepare for their own deaths as well.

Diaries and their composition still served as a bastion against the finality of death, even though accounts often end because either the writer or a loved one has died. By exhibiting the indelible stamp of each woman's existence and the ways in which she wished to present her being, diaries act as a monument to, and a recreation of, the life of their writer. British women's manuscript diaries are not the untidy, shapeless creations Virginia Woolf feared. Through their diverse subject matter and a variety of forms and styles, these diaries nonetheless exhibit recurrent patterns which indicate how each writer evaluated her milieu and herself, and chose to construct a record which mitigated against the chaos of death.

NOTES TO INTRODUCTION

[1] *A Writer's Diary* (New York: Harcourt Brace, 1953), p. 13.

[2] *A Literature of Their Own* (Princeton, N.J.: Princeton University Press, 1977), p. 9.

[3] Two scholars of women's studies who have most frequently expressed the need for more primary material are Elaine Showalter and Barbara Kanner. In "Feminist Criticism in the Wilderness" (*Writing and Sexual Difference*, ed. Elizabeth Abel [Chicago: University of Chicago Press, 1980], p. 35), Showalter emphasizes the necessity of examining what women actually wrote rather than dictate what women should write. Kanner indicates that theoretical interpretations of women's history should be linked to unexamined primary sources (Preface to *The Women of England: Interpretive Bibliographical Essays*, ed. Barbara Kanner [Hamden, Conn.: Archon Books, 1979], p. 2); and she specifically cites the usefulness of studying published diaries and journals and uncovering their manuscript counterparts ("The Women of England in a Century of Social Change: 1815-1914," in: *A Widening Sphere: Changing Roles of Victorian Women*, ed. Martha Vicinus

[Bloomington, Ind.: Indiana University Press, 1977], p. 219). For an excellent example of how diaries and autobiographies can illuminate social history, see Women and Philanthropy in 19th Century England, by F. K. Prochaska (Oxford: Clarendon Press, 1980).

[4] Robert A. Fothergill notes the emergence during the Victorian era of a large number of published diaries and comments that diarists would expect possibly to be published (Private Chronicles: A Study of English Diaries [London: Oxford University Press, 1974], pp. 32, 33). For references to the practice of reading manuscript diaries, see the subject index which accompanies this bibliography.

BRITISH WOMEN'S DIARIES:

A Descriptive Bibliography of Selected

Nineteenth-Century Women's Manuscript Diaries

A1.
BROUGHAM, LADY MARIANNE (b. 1785, d. 1865), University College Library, London. Brougham Papers, uncatalogued.
DATE AND LOCATION: 1798, 1806, 1809, 1815-63, with gaps. Hill Street, London; Paris; Italy; Brougham, Cumbria; Cheltenham, Gloucestershire; Hampton Court; Dover; Ramsgate, Kent; Brook Farm.
FORMAT: 20 volumes. The earlier volumes have printed formats while the later ones do not. The former are specially designed for ladies and contain such information as tables for pence and shillings, lists of the kings and queens of England, and catalogues of hackney coach fares. An integral part of the earlier volumes is their various entertainment features, for they contain poetry, stories, and songs, as well as enigmas, rebusses, and charades, which are answered in the succeeding year's volumes. Many of the stories are designed to impart a moral lesson. For instance, one narrative warns women against the blandishments of fortune hunters, while another presents a woman who wishes for the sake of her

lover that she was a virgin. The rebusses, charades, and enigmas are sometimes in French, and many of the songs are those sung at Vauxhall Gardens. The foldouts show a fashionable lady and a three-page spread depicting maternal affection.

In these volumes the same dates serve both for the writer's daily remarks and her keeping of accounts. Thus, the left-hand memoranda and observations page is divided horizontally into spaces meant to contain daily comments, while the right-hand accounts page is divided vertically into sections for amounts received and for money paid or lent, and then subdivided into columns marked pounds, shillings, and pence. The year, the month, the week, the number of days within the month, and the month's place within the year are printed at the top of the diary pages.

Many of the diarist's entries run over onto the accounts page because of the limited space available. She uses her early volumes to keep track of her donations to the poor and of her gambling expenses while at boarding school. These volumes are sporadically kept with a number of pages torn or cut out. Some comments are marked through.

The majority of the diaries are unprinted octavo volumes inscribed with the writer's name, the date, and the location. The entries are run together when the diarist first uses these volumes, although later she starts to space her comments. She sporadically writes the month and the location at the top of the page, and there are gaps in her generally daily entries. Some of her remarks about Lord Brougham are crossed through, and the volumes contain some blank pages. Occasionally she only enters the date. She includes maxims and useful addresses in the back of the volumes.

CONTENT: The many volumes maintained by Marianne Eden, widow of Thomas Spalding and wife of the Whig politician Henry Brougham, span much of her life. Her earliest volume briefly mentions her activities at boarding school, including her gambling, and notes as well visitors, the birthdays of her siblings, and the illuminations celebrating Nelson's victory. Interestingly, she writes about giving diaries as Christmas gifts, for the children each receive one from their father while they in turn present journals to the servants. One of the longest entries in her 1806 volume praises her deceased father; and when her brother John leaves for India, she contemplates never seeing him again. Her early diaries relate the events of her daily life, including her reading, and the visitors she receives. Her 1809 volumes principally tell of her recovery from ill health, presumably aided by restorative water taken at Cheltenham and by a regime of leeches. She often indicates at what time of the day she writes her journal, and she describes the high society she moves in during her Cheltenham sojourn.

Before the death of her first husband in 1815 her diary depicts the life of a London lady, for she describes opera and play performances, her walks and drives in Hyde Park and Kensington Gardens, and a round of balls. But her account becomes a typical travel diary when she goes to Italy and later to Paris to recover from the shock of her husband's death, which she deeply mourns. Her comments while traveling detail the accommodations, describe the places she visits, and reveal her xenophobia, as she finds foreigners uncouth and disagreeable. However, when she returns to London she unfavorably contrasts its social life to the Parisian whirl.

Her concerns in London are dominated by the behavior of her adolescent son Johnny, whose naughtiness is punished by the diarist's brother, and by her courtship with Lord Brougham. Although she considers Brougham fascinating, she is nevertheless distraught by her involvement with him because she fears social disapproval. She often addresses God after seeing Brougham; and she rather uncharacteristically applies a sermon exhorting the mending of errors to her own behavior. In the summer of 1819 she marries Brougham, already pregnant with his daughter. She records her daughter's birth in her diary as well as her protracted recovery from the delivery. Brougham's activities form an important part of her record even during her long illness; she mentions her children less often. Seven months after the birth, Lady Brougham attends her first ball and her life resumes its usual configuration, for she writes of going to the races and visiting estates. Occasionally she mentions political events, such as Brougham's speech defending Queen Caroline and the coronation of George IV.

In 1821 her two-year-old daughter dies only a few months before she gives birth to another daughter. She turns to God for support after her daughter's death, and although she has no obvious difficulty during the delivery of Brougham's second daughter, she experiences much pain after the birth. Her diary describes in some detail her problems with excessive milk and swollen breasts, and even after she feels she has recovered her health, she has relapses. Brougham does not tend to her during her illness, though when he is ill with a sore throat she attends him. Marianne Brougham frequently becomes sick after periods of nursing others, but when she is well her life follows a predictable pattern, since she resides either in London or at Brougham and participates in the usual activities of an aristocrat.

STYLISTIC FEATURES: Generally the entries are short, although if the diarist is distraught or noteworthy events have occurred, she writes more. She tends to write complete sentences but sometimes omits the personal pronoun. The sentence structure in her 1809 volumes is free-flowing and associational. She frequently uses French phrases to refer to unpleasant, unusual, or joyful circumstances, and she employs dots and dashes to express agitation and reserve. Occasionally she claims to be too unhappy to write. She makes some summaries after momentous events, such as childbirth or marriage.

A2.

VERULAM, LADY CHARLOTTE (b. 1783, d. 1863), Hertfordshire Record Office D/EU F78. See also Grimston, the Honorable Charlotte.

DATE AND LOCATION: November, 1809-May, 1814. Birkhampstead Castle, Gorhambury, Hertfordshire; London.

FORMAT: The large volume is covered with brown pasteboard, now cracked, and is inscribed by the diarist with her name. The pages of the volume are ruled vertically, with three columns on the left-hand side and one column on the right-hand side. The diarist has designated the left-hand columns as day of the week, day of the month, and the month and year. The location at which the diary was written is noted at the top of the page. Generally the entries are daily, although some of the days entered in the columns have no entries beside them.

CONTENT: Charlotte, Lady Verulam, was the first countess of Verulam, and the wife of James Walter Grimston, who was himself the fourth Viscount Grimston and the first Earl of Verulam. Her volume principally records the diarist's daily activities. Charlotte uses her diary to note the visitors at the Earl's Gorhambury estate, her attendance at church, the planting on the estate, her superintendence of a school, and most importantly, her children's progress. In the course of her record Charlotte gives birth to three children, and when the last of these dies, her journal entries end. She is very scrupulous about citing the state of her children's health--she writes down each tooth they cut, worries about protecting them from measles, and mentions the date of their weaning and vaccinations. Her diary also registers the state of her own health, notes the births of her children, her miscarriage, and the date of her recovery from childbirth. She also refers to churching after the birth of her children, as well as to the child's christening. Although her principal interest is her children, she also participates in a round of social activities. She visits other aristocratic homes and frequently attends the opera and balls. She describes the gala given by the Prince Regent to celebrate George III's birthday as a magnificent and very costly fete. She is concerned with important political events and those which impinge on her daily life. Consequently, she notes when her husband travels to London to attend the House of Lords. She also writes about the state of George III's health as a concern of Parliament, and expresses anxiety about the murder of Spencer Percival.

STYLISTIC FEATURES: The brief entries are longer when she describes the stately homes she visits. Her reference to herself as her children's mother and her continual use of the possessive "my" preceding any mention of her children indicates her strong maternal feelings. She employs formulaic expressions when she habitually thanks God for keeping her children from suffering.

A3.

GRIMSTON, HONORABLE CHARLOTTE (b. 1778, d. 1830), Hertfordshire Record Office D/EU F81-96. See also Verulam, Lady Charlotte.

DATE AND LOCATION: January, 1812-May?, 1829, with 1825 and 1827 volumes missing. Birkhampstead Castle, Gorhambury, Hertfordshire; London.

FORMAT: 15 volumes. The octavo pasteboard volumes have covers of either marbled or printed patterns, contain blank sheets, and are watermarked with a royal crest. The diarist uses one such volume per year and occasionally notes the month when she begins her sporadic entries, but most are only marked by the date.

The 1826 printed volume, which is entitled "The Private Diary," begins with an introduction explaining the advantages of keeping a diary, which include self-regulation and the remembrance of important personal and financial matters. The introduction explains that the appendix can be used for extracts of letters, accounts of particular transactions, and listings of principal events, so that the appendix can serve as a synopsis of the writer's life. The verso page of the 1826 volume shows entry divisions for the first four days of the week while the recto page contains spaces for Friday to Sunday with twice as much space alloted for Sunday.

CONTENT: The diary volumes kept by the Honorable Charlotte Grimston, the unmarried daughter of the third Viscount Grimston and the sister of Lord Verulam, report political events she has gleaned from newspaper accounts, list her readings, especially about botany, travel, and Hebrew, and recount conversations. She is particularly interested in the social and political life of the aristocracy, for her diary gives lengthy accounts of the activities of the Prince Regent and Queen Caroline, the murder of Prime Minister Percival, and the Catholic Question. Her concern with her own class is also shown in her painting and etching, as she constantly depicts royal women, whether alive or dead, and her accounts illustrate the marital problems aristocratic women face. She narrates the tale of a young aristocratic woman who was confined to one room until her husband's death, since neither member of the couple, who were betrothed to each other by their parents, could bear the presence of the other one.

She is especially fascinated with Napoleon and the French and closely follows their defeat by the British. In fact the latter part of several of her diary volumes narrate anecdotes of the French which reveal her xenophobia. She accuses Napoleon of ill-temper and barbarity when she tells of him slashing the table whenever his men failed immediately to understand his orders.

The volumes mention family events, particularly the births of her sister-in-law's numerous children, the activities of the local girls' Sunday School, and the celebrations of the common people, both in London and at Birkhampstead. In 1814 she describes the celebrations

on the frozen Thames and the Hyde Park fete honoring the centenary of the Hanoverian succession, as well as the local festivities in observance of peace. She fears the mob, demagogues such as Orator Hunt, and the spirit of revolution, which threaten the preservation of her class. In 1819 she refers to the ministers' proposals to curtail the freedom of the press and to prohibit public meetings; she feels both measures will preserve the aristocracy. Her first distinctly personal entry on 7 September 1817 describes her loss of sight and her accompanying feelings of pain; and the later volumes, which often contain large chronological gaps, mention her increasing infirmities and activities occurring on the estate, such as hunting.
STYLISTIC FEATURES: The entries are written in long, complicated sentences and contain narratives which feature dialogue and an omniscient point-of-view. Some of the sentences lack punctuation. The entries are sometimes short and at other times lengthy.

A4.
ARROWSMITH, LADY LOUISA (b. ?, d. 1840), Hertfordshire Record Office MS 70150-70168.
DATE AND LOCATION: 1818-20; 1822-32; 1836-37. Totteridge Park, Hertfordshire.
FORMAT: 17 volumes. The volumes are made of either pasteboard with marbled and colored covers or of morocco leather. Her entries are written daily and are demarcated by noting the date.

CONTENT: The volumes maintained by the wife of Edward Arrowsmith, an attorney to King's Bench and a churchwarden, describe the affairs of the estate, her interest in charity, and some current events. She often acts as her husband's legal secretary, and after his death she is the executor of his estate. She uses her journal to detail the running of the property, for she notes when animals are ill, comments about planting and haymaking, and remarks on sanitary measures such as the opening of drains and the emptying of cesspools. She always mentions the head of livestock sold at the annual Barnet Fair. Her diary sometimes serves as an account book, since she lists rents and expenditures, including some involving her extended family.

Charitable activities form a significant part of her life as she is involved in the running of the local girls' school, as well as in the distribution of bread and clothing to the poor. She describes the school children's special Christmas and New Year's dinners, notes the style of their catechism recital, and points out that time can be usefully employed in assisting others. She praises Britain for being God's agent because of the number of English missionaries and considers herself and others of her class as the Lord's distributors of charity. As her diary writing continues she becomes increasingly religious, for she records more about Sunday services, and each Christmas and New Year's she compares the bright beams of the sun to the splendor of God and

His creation and thanks God for His blessings.

The current events she reports in her journal range from the deaths and weddings of members of the royal family to the installation of gas lighting in the theater. She frequently includes her evaluation of plays or paintings, such as Haydon's, and describes panoramas in some detail. Her class bias is evident in her hatred and fear of the radicals whom she is convinced are prevented by divine intervention from destroying England. Consequently, her record includes derogatory comments about Orator Hunt and a long description of the Cato Street conspirators and their execution. She eulogizes George III at the time of his death and writes about the coronation of George IV and the wedding of Princess Elizabeth.

Her husband died in 1827. The diarist writes long detailed descriptions of the physical symptoms which result in his death, as well as a eulogy to him and comments about her duty to her husband and to God. She notes who was present at the opening of her husband's will and at his funeral, and she offers thanks to God for preserving her through the affliction of his death. One of her longer entries features the detailed description of a monument to a dying wife. The dying woman is surrounded by her family members, who are resigned to her death and anxious not to disturb her meeting with her Maker. Among the sculpted figures only her sister offers the sufferer any solace. The monument illustrates the acceptance of death, and possibly also the way women comforted each other on such occasions.

STYLISTIC FEATURES: Her entries differ in length and generally lack punctuation to separate sentences. The entries are longer when she is describing interesting sights such as the panoramas, or significant events such as the Cato Street Conspiracy. She sometimes refers to women as the "female part." In times of distress or at the end of the year she addresses God directly, and increasingly she notes the texts of sermons. Only rarely does she comment that there is nothing particular to write.

A5.
DE RUTZEN, BARONESS (b. ?, d. ?), National Library of Wales, Slebech 2, 993.
DATE AND LOCATION: August-October, circa 1820-30. Paris.
FORMAT: The diary fragment is made up of large, loose sheets of paper folded into smaller pages to make a petite volume. The entries are daily.
CONTENT: This diary details the activities of a woman who moved in aristocratic circles. She uses her handmade volume to catalogue hiring servants, writing letters, and attending costume balls and church. She also employs it to keep track of the weather and to note who called or attended a party. This typical diary of an aristocratic woman mentions the Princess of Denmark; its unusual make-up symbolizes the strong impulse to write a unified

volume which the diary form can engender.

STYLISTIC FEATURES: The short entries are written in fragments.

A6.

ASHTON, MARIANNE (b. ?, d. ?), National Library of Wales, Harpton Court 2, 743.

DATE AND LOCATION: 1824. Paris; Switzerland; England; Ireland.

FORMAT: The green pasteboard, pocket volume French diary has leather oblong rings attached to the inside of the front and back covers, so that when the diary is closed it has the appearance of being bound on that side. The cost of items in francs is scribbled on the first few pages of plain white paper, as is the inscription signifying that this is a gift of Lord Epit.

This printed pocket volume contains information in French, such as listings of cab fares, Saints' days, and French ministers, and comparisons of new and old measurements and of French and foreign currency. There are spaces for two entries per page with the month, date, day, and its significance printed at the top of the page or entry.

CONTENT: This 1824 pocket diary was used to keep track of expenditures and travels. Judging from the entries, its owner was an aristocrat. The few entries before July 24 list the amounts spent for carriages and presumably for servants. Between July 24 and September 9, the entry spaces are filled with typical travel comments about the scenery, the meals, the distances traveled, and the places visited during the diarist's Swiss tour. Between September 28 and October 11 the diarist uses her pocket book to list similar details about her trip between Lausanne and London. Her final entries mention her travels to Hampton Court and to Dublin on October 20.

STYLISTIC FEATURES: The fragmentary entries are written in English in both ink and pencil.

A7.

DENMAN, FRANCES (b. 1812, d. 1890), Wigan Record Office M975 EHC 183.

DATE AND LOCATION: July, 1832-April, 1833. Russell Square, London; Isle of Wight; the Midlands; Derbyshire.

FORMAT: The half-bound, leather volume has marbled covers; it is apparently the second volume of a sequence. On the inside front cover the diarist has written the date of her grandmother's death, the date she commenced her journal, and a list of the books she read while keeping her diary. The books include <u>She Stoops to Conquer</u>, <u>Evelina</u>, and several by Harriet Martineau. Her entries are marked with the day and date, and the month is listed at the top of the page; generally she writes daily entries, though she also sometimes composes a running narrative of several weeks. The entries are spotty during the last month of the diary.

CONTENT: The diary written by Frances Denman, one of the

eleven children of Lord Chief Justice Thomas Denman, represents the life of a young lady in London and her visits to relatives throughout England. She uses her diary to record bits of conversation either she or her father hear during dinner parties and to recount unusual and intriguing narratives of people's lives. Often the narratives contain a moral message; for example, one recounts an aristocrat who, because of her father's neglect of her education, married badly and met a violent death through accidental poisoning. Such a tale is reminiscent of those in Victorian penny weeklies, where parental neglect also brings the children misfortune and ruin. The diary contains numerous descriptions of people she encounters, particularly of women, and there is a lengthy account as well of William IV proroguing Parliament. Her comments on her reading, which includes the Bible, Don Quixote, and Pilgrim's Progress, usually center on her evaluation of female characters.

She frequently reads to others, especially her father, and her entries indicate his importance in the household. When her father is at home the diarist records all of his activities, and the women stop practising the piano. Frances is a very obedient daughter who much admires her father. During the course of the diary he becomes the Lord Chief Justice, and she writes how delighted she is that all her father's friends are so sincerely happy about his success. The diary includes some commentary about political matters, such as the Irish

Reform Bill and the possibility of war with Holland, usually because her father reports news about politics as well as about the law. One of his principal friends is Lord Brougham.

The diarist's ordinary activities include music lessons, evening entertainments, and social visits. During one round of calls, Frances becomes frustrated while she waits idly in the carriage for her mother, and then chastizes herself for her inappropriate behavior and her misuse of time. Her recounting of the evening entertainments notes the members of the company and the games played. She discusses the manner in which marriage proposals should be made, describes her fondness for her music teacher, and notes the beauty of her grandmother's face in death. Although she was unmarried while she kept this volume, she married Admiral Sir Robert Lambert Baynes in 1846.

STYLISTIC FEATURES: Sometimes she omits the subject of the sentence, and in such cases it can be difficult to decide whether she is referring to her father or herself. There is considerable variation in entry length. If few events have occurred or, conversely, if she is very much occupied as she is during the social season, she writes very little. However, when she narrates anecdotes her entries are quite long, and her ability as a storyteller is evident in these entries. She uses dialogue and phraseology which indicate voice quality and intonation.

A8.

MILFORD, LADY (b. ?, d. 1852), National Library of Wales, Picton Castle 607. See also De Rutzen, Baroness.

DATE AND LOCATION: 1839-44, with large gaps. Portland Place, London; Picton Castle, near Carmarthen, Wales.

FORMAT: The large, thick volume has a locking clasp and black leather covers edged in gilt. The diarist occasionally summarizes several months and omits writing during her travels.

CONTENT: The diary of Baron Milford's wife details her daily life in London and to a lesser extent at Picton Castle. A friend of Baroness de Rutzen, she participates in the usual activities of her class, for she records her outings in the phaeton; the hiring and firing of servants; attendance at royal functions, dinner parties, the theater and the opera; and journeys by train to the spa, or on the yacht. Much of her time is spent driving with her husband to the House of Lords or Brooker's Club. She reports his political endeavors, especially if he stays late at the House of Lords to hear an important debate.

Either she or her husband are often ill, so frequently the diary catalogues his symptoms of gout and rheumatism. Her journal gives her reactions to the performances of celebrities such as Kean and Macready, and to the ceremonies surrounding the marriage and the birthday observances of Queen Victoria. Her acquisition of a pet poodle is a notable event, as is her discharging of the footman for telling a dreadful story.

STYLISTIC FEATURES: The diary is written in long, fairly complex sentences, which often omit the personal pronoun.

A9.

CAPEL, LADY ADELA (b. 1828, d. 1860), Hertfordshire Record Office D/Z 32 F1.

DATE AND LOCATION: April, 1841-April, 1842. Eglinton Castle, Ayrshire, Scotland; London.

FORMAT: The volume has marbled pasteboard covers and a black spine. The publishers of this <u>1841 Richards's Universal Daily Remembrancer</u> advertise it as an annual diary, which includes memoranda, bills due, appointments, and an almanac, and claim it is useful to attorneys, bankers, merchants, architects, auctioneers, military men, and gentlemen. Its contents comprise listings of army and navy agents, London and country bankers, British and foreign ambassadors, directors of the East India Company, the Lord Mayor and Aldermen of London, judges, Lord Lieutenants in England and Wales, archbishops and bishops, the members of the Houses of Lords and Commons, and the royal family. It also contains information about assessed taxes, commercial and law stamps, hackney coach fares, life and fire insurance, mail routes, meetings of literary and scientific institutions, and universities. There are tables to calculate wages and interest, to assess taxes, and to show the probable duration of life. The pages are divided into quarters with the last space designated as occasional memoranda, so that a week is shown when the diary is opened. Since the diarist employs the first part of the volume for 1842, rather than 1841, she crosses out the printed days and inserts the correct ones for 1842. She writes daily.

CONTENT: The diary maintained by the fourteen-year-old daughter of the 6th Earl of Eglinton, shows her love of animals and gardening. The 1841 section of her record describes the devotion of her pet fawn, Fairy, and the fawn's unfortunate death from distemper. Adela tenderly mourns Fairy's death by visiting her grave and writing verses, which appear at the back of the volume. When she travels to London in 1842, she inquires about getting another fawn, and she mentions that she intends to raise a pet lamb until she can procure a fawn. Adela uses her account to note her London activities, which include shopping and attending "The Marriage of Figaro," just as she employs her diary to record her pursuits while in the country. Much of her time is spent taking care of numerous birds and rabbits. She mentions enjoying reading a travel journal about southern Ireland, and wishes that she had a sister as a companion, since she likes playing with girls.

STYLISTIC FEATURES: Her sentences are run together and not punctuated, and there are occasional misspellings. The entries are of medium length. She records weather conditions in the space for occasional memoranda.

ARISTOCRACY

A10.

COWPER, LADY ADINE (b. 1843, d. 1868), Hertfordshire Record Office MS Ref. AR 1287 Panshanger Box 37; MS. Ref. 1627.

DATE AND LOCATION: August, 1857-August, 1861; 1866; 1868. London; Paris; Panshanger, near Hertford; Wrest Park, Bedfordshire; Isle of Wight; Lynton, Devon.

FORMAT: Three volumes. The first extant volume, which is written from 1857-61, is bound in black leather and inscribed with the diarist's name, the date, the location, and a notation that this is the second volume. The sporadic entries list the day of the week and the date at the left-hand edge of the page, and mark as well the time of day during which events occur. Each month is demarcated only at its inception.

Both the 1866 and the 1868 pocketbook volumes are printed and contain listings of law and university terms, public holidays, stamp duties, post office regulations, London bankers, and assessed taxes. Both the 1866 and 1868 volumes have spaces for four entries per page; the month and year are printed at the top of each page. The cash accounts section in both volumes contains pages for each month, which are divided into spaces for entering items and for keeping track of the amount in pounds, shillings, and pence of these items. In both printed volumes the diarist keeps sporadically daily entries and writes additional comments in the space at the bottom of the right-hand page provided for these. She divides entries by consistently noting the time of day during which activities occur. In the 1866 volume she uses the cash accounts section to expand some entries while in the 1868 diary this section is principally employed to keep track of the cost of books. The blank pages at the beginning of the 1868 volume, which are labeled by the diarist "Pre-Appendix," relate her sojourn in Cambridge. She writes very few entries from the time of her son's birth in 1868 until her death a few months later.

CONTENT: The diary maintained by the daughter of George Augustus Frederick, the 6th Earl of Cowper, and later the wife of Julian Henry Charles Fane, depicts her girlhood as well as her life as a young woman and mother. Her perceptive account of her girlhood from 1857 to 1861 indicates her awareness of the insensitivity expressed by the aristocracy towards the poor, as well as her realization of the inferior position of women. She often speculates what she would do if she were a man, a form of fantasy in which her sisters also indulge, and states that because women are treated so badly she believes the adage that a woman's happiest moment is her death. She prefers village men to gentlemen, whom she considers false, and protests against the unfair division of monetary and social advantages as well as the labeling by the rich of the poor as animals.

Her unhappiness with the milieu of the nineteenth century causes her to turn to the Middle Ages, which she considers heroic, and to reading, her favorite activity.

Although she studies medieval church architecture and religious painting, she is especially fond of poetry and peruses Milton, Coleridge, Shakespeare, Longfellow, Byron, Schiller, Lessing, Dante, and Tennyson. Her critiques of her reading and sermons are virtually always positive. She admires Tennyson as much as she does the local clergyman, her older brother Henry, and her dead father. She respects all men who are ascetics. She would like to be either a clergyman or a martyr, but considers herself too fond of approbation to be an exemplary Christian. Her 1857-61 volume becomes increasingly concerned with religious belief and her growing adherence to Catholicism.

Much of her time is spent dispensing charity. She mentions some political events, such as the war in Italy and the opening of China to Europeans. After her brother starts a volunteer unit to fight a French invasion, she frequently mentions its activities just as she writes of reading her sister's diary and of the love she feels for her siblings and her best friend. Although she is fond of her intimates, she hates aristocratic society in general and compares girls' position in it to a sick room.

Her 1866 and 1868 volumes express some of the same concerns as her earlier volume, though the later ones are less reflective and more apt simply to record daily activities. In her 1866 accounts she frequently writes of Gladstone and reform and refers to her soul as middle-class because she dislikes hearing "fearfully aristocratic utterances." Like other London ladies, she rides in the park and visits exhibitions, but she loathes balls and the London social season. She signifies her wedding day in 1866 by only writing her married name, Adine Fane. Her 1868 volume comments on her children and reading, especially of American newspapers. There is only a brief mention of her son's birth in 1868, presumably because she died only a few months after it.

STYLISTIC FEATURES: In the 1857-61 volume the entry lengths vary, depending on the extent of the diarist's reflective comments and the occurrence of narratives about the activities of noble men. Often she writes long sentences, and she sometimes omits the first person personal pronoun, especially if she is noting daily activities. She directly addresses God in times of spiritual need and self-examination, and she uses dots to refer to prostitutes. She crosses out some of her remarks both to correct errors and to revise. She adds some additional comments between sentences. She often refers to the weather as a "lotus-eating" day.

The entries in the 1866 and 1868 volumes are short and cryptic. At the time of her marriage her comments become briefer and her handwriting more indecipherable. Both the later volumes are written in a small, cramped, illegible hand.

A11.

REYNOLDS, LADY R. (Mrs. Frances Crepigny), (b. ?, d. ?),

Hertfordshire Record Office MS Reference 86135.

DATE AND LOCATION: 1859-64, with gaps. London; Paris; Switzerland; Cheltenham, Gloucestershire; Gosport, Hampshire; Isle of Wight.

FORMAT: The pocketbook, black leather volume has gold trim and lined pages. The volume is inscribed "Frances Ch. Crepigny," for at the time the diary was written the author was Mrs. Frances Crepigny. Her entries have gaps between November, 1860, and May, 1861, between June and August, 1861, between December, 1861, and April, 1862, and between October, 1862, and March, 1863. The entries become fewer and fewer between June, 1863, and March, 1864, when the diary ends.

CONTENT: This record kept by a well-to-do woman details her daily activities in London, as well as her pursuits abroad and in England. Although Lady Reynolds resided in London, she traveled frequently. Her entries during her sojourns mention the sights she visited, the accommodations she rented, and the food she ate. She begins her diary when she leaves London for Paris where she goes to the almost completed tomb of Napoleon, often walks in the Bois de Boulogne, and frequently attends the opera. She visits French chateaus as well as English country houses, and she notes what is unusual or of primary interest about the sights she sees. For example, she describes in some detail the stained glass windows in Rouen Cathedral.

Her London activities entail frequent outings with

her son Charlie when he is home from school. She goes
to the British Museum, the National Gallery, the Royal
Academy, and the Crystal Palace. She seems fond of visiting flower exhibitions and cattle and dog shows. She
uses her diary to note who called, to mention her walks
and drives in the parks, to record whom she hears preach
in which church, and to cite her attendance at balls, the
opera, and the theater. When she does not leave the
house she records her visitors, but she never writes down
what pursuits she follows at home. When she is in Cheltenham she writes nothing in her diary.

STYLISTIC FEATURES: The very brief entries give little
of the diarist's reactions to events. The entries are
slightly longer when the diarist leaves home. She tends
to write full sentences in a bold but almost illegible
hand.

A12.

LASCELLES, HONORABLE FREDERICA (b. 1848, d. 1891), Wigan
Record Office, MS 999 EHC 199.

DATE AND LOCATION: 1885. London; Lancashire.

FORMAT: The black pasteboard volume with an engraved
spine was published by Houghton and Grimm. It contains
advertisements for other products from the publisher,
such as menus and visiting cards, and registers of game,
wine, and household accounts. The advertisements at the
back of the volume feature a writing cabinet, a stationery
case and blotting book combination, and a small grand-

father clock. This volume includes information about
foreign currency and postage, Indian parcel post, and
passports, in addition to the usual notations of Sunday
lessons and the terms at Oxford and Cambridge. The format is unusual because it displays pages with columns
designed to help the user keep track of books and articles
lent. The pages are ruled and show the day, month, and
date at the top of the page. Occasionally the diarist
skips an entry, but on the whole she writes daily.
CONTENT: The volume, kept by the wife of the Honorable
Frederick Canning Lascelles, was an 1884 Christmas present which the diarist primarily employed to record the
activities of the family and the servants. She notes the
servants' wages and their terms of employment, and she
mentions the illnesses, marriages, and deaths in her
family. Her four daughters figure largely in her account,
for the diarist teaches them to write, read, and speak
French. She escorts her children to plays and birthday
parties as well. She is very involved in the Mission
League. She is also concerned with letting the family's
London residence, which she helps refurbish by taking up
the floorcloth in the nursery. She records the children's
height and weight, notes her birthday and the anniversary
of her wedding seven years earlier, and comments on the
peaceful death of her father. A change in government
ruins her husband's prospects for a post as Inspector of
Fisheries. The family visits friends in Lancashire where
the men shoot and play cricket. The diarist often men-

tions the weather and comments on certain political events, such as Gordon's involvement in Khartoum. She records that after the massacre took place there, the evening papers were edged in black.

STYLISTIC FEATURES: The brief entries are written in elliptical sentence fragments. The diarist frequently uses dashes.

A13.

LYTTON, LADY EDITH (b. 1842, d. 1936), Hertfordshire Record Office MS Reference 57462.

DATE AND LOCATION: April-May, 1893. Paris.

FORMAT: The daily account is written on nineteen pages of unbound stationery. The diarist's pencil inscription on the front indicates that the diary is about her arrival in Paris and that the account will be kept by her.

CONTENT: The wife of Edward Robert Lytton, the son of the novelist Edward George Bulwer-Lytton and the first Earl of Lytton, wrote her diary during her husband's tenure in Paris as First Secretary at the British Embassy. She begins her account by expressing regret about leaving her children who remain in England. She gets ill during the crossing, and although she is initially told there are no cabins available, she feels she is later given one because of the effect of her title upon the vulgar. Her xenophobia consistently informs her diary: she records that the scrubby appearance and bad manners of the French aristocracy increase her sense of her own aristocratic

breeding; and her final entry declares the superiority
of English art to French painting. She especially dislikes the impropriety of the badly painted nude women she
sees at an exhibition in Paris. She constantly voices
her displeasure about being snubbed diplomatically. She
uses her diary to note who calls, her visits to the theater and the sights of Paris, plans for renting a house
in Paris, and her shopping expeditions. She finds Paris
an excellent place to shop. She occasionally mentions
her husband's duties at the embassy; for instance, she
writes that he is told by the French that the British
government is behaving badly over the Suez Canal.
STYLISTIC FEATURES: The long entries are written in
complete, fairly complex sentences and clearly express
the diarist's bias toward England and the English.

G1.
STEWART, MRS. (b. ?, d. ?), National Library of Scotland
MS 982.
DATE AND LOCATION: February-December, 1802, with gaps.
Bonskeid, Scotland.
FORMAT: The large red volume has been rebound. A page
of contents correlates this diary with a list contained
in the National Library of Scotland MS. 982.

The diary is kept daily for about the first week.
There are no entries between February 8 and May 23 when
the diarist composes a summary entry. After this date
the diary is kept regularly, although the writer fails

to date each entry. Instead she dates entries weekly, but not on a given day, and then differentiates succeeding entries by noting the day of the week. There is no spacing between the entries, and by August she is again writing summary entries.

CONTENT: The diary, which is kept by an apparently widowed Scottish gentlewoman, reports the activities of her circle and presents amusing narratives which reflect both her milieu and the writer's wry humor. One of her most revealing anecdotes involves her own chagrin when she loses her petticoat on the road after church and has to use her friend as a screen. She realizes the discrepancy between appearance and reality, particularly in relations between the sexes, for she tells the story of a husband who considered himself deceived when he discovered his wife used rouge.

Conscious of fashion, she mentions in detail what is worn in London, and how women of her acquaintance dress. She also uses her diary to comment on her reading; for example, she makes brief remarks about her perusal of biographies of illustrious ladies. Because she is superstitious, her writings reveal the customs of her age, such as the consumption of seed cakes by newlyweds to help them dream of each other.

STYLISTIC FEATURES: The entry length depends on the amount the diarist has to relate. The writer is a good storyteller of the dramatic and humorous events she encounters or hears about. The handwriting is unclear and there are some misspellings.

G2.

DAVIS, MISS (b. ?, d. ?), Wigan Record Office M847 EHC 78. DATE AND LOCATION: This is a photocopied and bound version of the original 1810 volume of the <u>Ladies' Complete Pocket Book</u>. The contents include listings of hackney coach fares, transfer days at the Bank, public offices, and members of the royal family, as well as tables for marketing and casting up expenses. The 1810 pocket book features answers to the enigmas and rebusses printed in the previous year's volume, as well as new enigmas, rebusses, Vauxhall songs, and country dances. Many of the pages at the volume's end, which contained this new material, were not photocopied.

The volume is designed so that memoranda and observations are to be written on the verso page, which has days of the week and dates running down its left side. The recto page is designated for accounts, and has columns for paid and received, which are divided into spaces for pounds, shillings, and pence. On the accounts pages are printed the month, the number of days and weeks in the month, and the current week of the month. The writer used the memorandum pages at the beginning of the diary to keep track of what was owed her, and, conversely, of her debts. She often employed the accounts page to note visitors. The poor quality photocopy makes many of the entries difficult to read.

CONTENT: The diary kept by a well-connected unmarried woman notes her social engagements and activities. She was involved in sailing and in the regatta and she enjoyed sea-bathing. She mentions births, the King's illness, the weather, and a visit to Lytham.

STYLISTIC FEATURES: The entries are very brief and sporadically kept. Toward the end of the volume the entries deal more with the diarist's activities and less with accounts.

G3.

POLHILL, FRANCES M. (b. 1802, d. ?), Hertfordshire Record Office D/P78 29/1.

DATE AND LOCATION: January-December 1836, with gaps. London; Howbury Hall, Bedfordshire.

FORMAT: The volume, which has a green cover and red binding, is embossed with the date and is inscribed by the diarist with her name and the date. This <u>Law and Commercial Daily Remembrancer</u> contains listings of London fire engine establishments, public notaries, post office regulations, holidays at public offices, poor law commissioners, hackney coach fares, and governors of British colonies, as well as an analysis of the eighty-four acts passed in the 5th and 6th William IV Parliamentary sessions. There are also tables of weights and measures and of interest at four and five per cent. The contents note the duties on hair powder as well as on dogs. A section for monthly summaries was not used by the diarist. There is a half-page space for each day's entry and the same amount of space for the memoranda entry. The date and day of the month, as well as notable information, are printed at the top of the page. The volume is spottily maintained, since there are no entries between February and March and between November and December. In the occasional memoranda section for January the diarist mentions the extreme coldness of the weather, and in the observations section she lists some expenses.

CONTENT: The journal of the wife of Frederick Polhill, a Member of Parliament, records Frances's daily activities and ends with comments about her nearly fatal illness. Many of her remarks concern her four children, three of whom are away at school. The diarist goes to the dancing academy to see her daughters perform, and when the children are on holiday she accompanies them to London sights and to church. Her journal also notes her husband's presence at the Bedford Assizes and records her own attendance at London amusements, such as the theater and a watercolor exhibition. She employs her diary to keep track of the coming and going of servants, the visits of friends, business transactions, and occasionally her own unhappiness. Her mother-in-law dies in the course of Frances's record, but it is the diarist's own illness from inflammation of the chest which causes much more comment, for she notes having seventeen leeches applied to her hair and being expected to die.

STYLISTIC FEATURES: The brief entries concisely list the

diarist's daily activities by using sentence fragments. The entries which deal with her illness are written after her recovery, and these emphatically depict her condition through exclamation points and her thanks to God for renewed health.

G4.

ESTCOURT, MARIANNE HARRIET (b. 1814, d. 1885), Gloucestershire Record Office D1571, F555-8.

DATE AND LOCATION: 1841-46; 1853-56. London; Gloucester; Derbyshire; France; Italy; the Crimea.

FORMAT: Four volumes. The first two diary volumes have marbled pasteboard covers with leather surfaces and spines, while the third and fourth volumes have dark purple leather covers. All four volumes are unusual because they can be locked. At the back of the first volume there are loose prayers, poems, notes on sermons, and newspaper clippings concerning the Canadian Boundary commission of her brother James. The third and fourth volumes include reports about the Crimea.

CONTENT: The first two diary volumes, which were kept by the unmarried daughter of a doctor and landowner, depict her life between 1841 and 1846 as her father's secretary and as a teacher at a day school for poor children. Much of her time is spent settling accounts or writing letters, and she uses her diary to bemoan the tedium of these duties, as well as to narrate anecdotes such as that of a woman who carries about the ashes of her beloved dog. She also employs her journal to assess her character, especially on her birthday, for she is continually anxious to be more religious. Marianne Estcourt recounts her uncle's death and other deathbed scenes, evidently as an aid to her own religiosity. She comments on the status of unmarried women: for example, she quotes approvingly Wilberforce's view that the lot of unwed women has improved because they can now assist the poor.

She describes her extensive reading and makes observations about maintaining a diary. In her earliest volume she begins by writing that this is the first time she has committed the extravagance of buying a journal with a lock. She quotes a friend who says it is impossible to keep a journal because we never justly judge ourselves. She also mentions hearing a friend's diary read aloud.

The third and fourth volumes describe the travels of the diarist and her sister-in-law, Caroline; more importantly they depict conditions in the Crimea and the death of her brother James in 1855. The parts of the diary which recount the journeys of Marianne and Caroline include details which are standard for travelogues, for they record sights visited, assess hotel accommodations, and note particular customs. The diarist intersperses sketches throughout her commentary and observes the anniversaries of both parents' deaths.

The entries about her visits to the Crimea are

fascinating since they portray wretched hospital conditions and important battles, including the Charge of the Light Brigade. The diarist finds Florence Nightingale cold and overbearing and depicts the problems created by the influx of soldiers' wives. The heartrending, meticulous description of James's death from cholera includes graphic details of the progress of the disease, as well as a rendering of the emotions experienced by his wife and sister, both of whom witnessed his death. The diarist connects the anniversary of her mother's death with James's, which occurs only a day later, and records the solace she offers Caroline during their mutual mourning. The third and fourth volumes vividly portray the Crimean War since they comprise not only the diarist's personal comments, but also newspaper accounts, diagrams of battles, and extracts from letters.

STYLISTIC FEATURES: The detailed commentary distinctly expresses the diarist's point-of-view. The entries of the first two volumes are either lengthy or terse, depending on her state of mind. Her observations about the Crimea are descriptive and illuminating.

G5.
RUSSELL, MISS HELEN (b. 1835?, d. ?), National Library of Scotland MS. 3233.
DATE AND LOCATION: November, 1854-March, 1855. Ashiesteel, Borders, Scotland.
FORMAT: The large pasteboard volume contains pages with

the month and year written at the top by the diarist.
The dates and day of the week are listed at the beginning
of the daily entries. The first two pages are half torn
off.

CONTENT: The diary of a young lady whose father succeeded Sir Walter Scott at the Ashiesteel estate in Scotland details her round of social and domestic activities both at the country estate and in Edinburgh. Her account includes some mention of political events, such as the Crimean War and the death of the Czar. Like other young ladies, Helen Russell attends balls, the opera, lectures, and charity bazaars, and engages in handiwork, drawing, and singing. Her class bias is apparent when she refers to the workers not suffering from the cold, as do members of the upper class.

An especially interesting feature of her journal is the extent to which it reflects the importance of keeping diaries. She is obviously in the habit of keeping one herself as this volume is simply her most recent one; she refers to reading published and manuscript diaries, discussing them with her friends, and the practice by others of keeping diaries. Her close relationship with her cousin Julia is maintained by their reading each other's diaries.

STYLISTIC FEATURES: The diary is regularly written in sentence fragments. The writer typically begins an entry by mentioning the weather and then relates the day's activities, which can serve as a starting point for more extended observations. Parts of some entries are written in code.

G6.

FULLER, MRS. JULIANA (b. ?, d. ?), Wigan Record Office M993 EHC 195.

DATE AND LOCATION: 1866; 1867; 1868. Bath and Devon; Switzerland; Wales.

FORMAT: The album volume contains illustrations of the diarist and her husband's three trips. The first journey, in 1866, was a honeymoon sojourn in Bath and Devon; the second, in 1867, was a holiday in Switzerland; and the third, in 1868, was a vacation in Wales. The album includes photographs, postcards, sketches, pressed flowers and seaweed, and locks of hair, all of which help depict the couple, their residences, and their travels. The entries are daily.

CONTENT: The diary of three travelogues was kept by the daughter of John D. Taylor, Esq., of Grovelands, Middlesex, and the wife of John Stratton Fuller, Esq., of Hyde House, Chesham, Buckinghamshire. It begins with a brief mention of the leave-taking after her wedding. She notes the couple's activities during their honeymoon trip. Interestingly, she reads in the sitting room while her husband goes walking because the couple could not procure a donkey for her to ride. The account of their wedding tour ends with the diarist's comments about their joyful return home to apartments newly furnished by friends and relatives, and to a celebration which featured singing and hand bell playing.

Her recounting of the journey to Switzerland describes the sights visited by the couple, but it is also a reminiscence for the diarist, since she had visited the Alps as a child. Again, her husband goes out while she remains indoors, and the insistence that she ride rather than walk indicates the physical constraints of female roles. The diarist sketches during her Swiss tour, as she does during her Welsh one. The couple's holiday in Wales is characterized by a trip to Tintern Abbey and their frequent church attendance. Generally the entries simply relate the sights they visited.
STYLISTIC FEATURES: The habitual use of "we" rather than "I" indicates that this diary is not a personal record but an account of the couple's travels together. The diarist often employs the superlative to describe scenery, and this tendency, along with the inclusion of photographs and sketches, gives the record the effect of a travel brochure.

G7.
LLWYNGWAIN, HARRIETTE BOWEN (b. ?, d. ?), National Library of Wales, Llwyngwain 17, 233-34.
DATE AND LOCATION: 1886-87. Near Cardigan, Wales.
FORMAT: Two volumes. The 1886 volume is an <u>Army and Navy Pocket Diary</u> with a gray pressboard cover, with "Diary 1886" embossed in gilt. The contents include

listings of anniversaries, remarkable events, holidays, battles, London bankers, London daily and weekly papers, dates for sportsmen, and post office data. Under the section regarding stamp duties there is information about the cost to the custodian of a lunatic, and under the assessed taxes section the fees for dogs are listed. The 1886 volume advertises other Army and Navy Co-operative Society goods, such as various types of pocket diaries. At the back of this volume there is a section for cash accounts, and at the front there are memoranda pages.

On the left-hand page there are spaces for Monday to Wednesday, along with the respective dates, while on the right-hand page the remaining four days and dates appear. The month and year are printed at the top of each page with Biblical lessons cited under the Sunday entry, which has almost no space for writing. The right-hand side of each page exhibits spaces for the diarist to enter expenditures in pounds, shillings, and pence.

The 1887 volume is similar to the 1886 tome in appearance and contents, though the former is a Pettitt's Annual Diary. The 1887 volume contains several illuminating items. For instance, it notifies parents that their children should be registered within forty-two days after birth and informs relatives that deaths should be reported within five days. It has advertisements for other types of diaries and books, including the Improved Family Washing Book, the Handy Diary, and the Housekeeper's Memorandum book. Other advertisements attempt to sell bottled remedies, typewriters, and subscriptions to the Married Law Defense Union, whose particular purpose is to resist the legalization of marriage with a wife's sister. Many dates have no entries.

CONTENT: These 1886 and 1887 diaries of a well-to-do woman who appears to be running a large household are excellent examples of printed diaries and of their use to keep track of accounts and appointments. In the 1886 volume the diarist lists items and prices, especially under the cash accounts section. Her entries confine themselves to notations of who was invited to dinner or parties, when the children returned to school, dates of penny readings, elections, theater performances, railway openings, and Primrose Society meetings (the Conservative Party women's group). In the 1887 volume more fiscal accounts are included in the entry spaces, though she also mentions the weather, balls, rents due, and deaths. Both volumes are good sources for the cost of everyday items such as spectacle cases, playing cards, stockings, and beer.

STYLISTIC FEATURES: The listings are terse and the entries are written in fragments.

PC1. HASLAM, SARAH? (b. 1750, d. 1815?), Wigan Record Office M969 EHC 177.

DATE AND LOCATION: August-October, 1802. Welsh tour from and to London.

FORMAT: The leather-bound, oblong, clasped volume contains watercolors of castle ruins, churches, and landscapes, all painted by the diarist. There are blank pages at the end of the volume. Early entries summarize several days; later entries are daily. The dates are entered in the margins.

CONTENT: The travel diary, which allegedly belonged to Sarah Haslam, the daughter of Colonel Haslam and later the second wife of John Eardley-Wilmot, was maintained during a family journey to Wales, Oxford, Blenheim, Ross-on-Wye, and Cheltenham. The account of the tour disparages the revival of Gothic architecture, while it lauds the beauties of nature. The drawings add to the diarist's praise of natural scenery, for they depict sublime views of rocks and mountains. She particularly criticizes the buildings James Wyatt constructed for Lord Carrington, since she feels their architectural variety is excessive and in conflict with modern customs. She often comments on the group's guides, one of whom was a poor woman, who was clothed in rags and nursed several children. The diarist graphically describes this poor woman's wretched existence and comments that the luxuries obtained by the rich through rents are bought too dearly when they are purchased by means of such suffering.

STYLISTIC FEATURES: The heightened prose is replete with the conceits of eighteenth-century poetic diction. Through a skillful use of language, the diarist forcefully expresses her opinions.

PC2.

STUART, T. (b. ?, d. ?), Wigan Record Office M828 EHC 159.

DATE AND LOCATION: July 1813; July 1814; 1825-34. Durham to Bath; Bath to Weymouth.

FORMAT: The volume has stiff marbled covers and contains some interesting memoranda, such as a page of historical anecdotes about silk manufacturing, an excerpt entitled "The History of Women," an advertisement featuring a testimonial about a cure for breast cancer, and a poem deriding Napoleon. The entries made during her travels are not designated by date, but rather by the day of the journey, such as second day, third day, etc. The records of her Bible reading cite when she commenced and finished reading. The diary also contains some housekeeping accounts.

CONTENT: The diary of a young wife and mother begins in July, 1813, when the family moves from Durham, their previous residence which the writer regretted leaving. Although her account of their two July journeys is chiefly a description of accommodations and meals, she makes some interesting remarks about two factories they visited. The establishment where silk was manufactured employed several hundred girls, and the other, which produced imitation Turkish carpets, was staffed by women and children. The diarist dislikes Napoleon, and she comments about the celebrations of Wellington's victory over him. Her notations of her Bible readings indicate that she felt she needed spiritual aid.

STYLISTIC FEATURES: The travelogue entries are primarily descriptive and include sufficient detail to present a clear picture. The tone of her accounts of bible reading is piously resigned. The later entries indicate a significant change in the diarist, for the earlier notations make no mention of religion.

PC3.

HOLTZAPFEL, CHARLOTTE (b. 1800, d. 1873), Wigan Record Office D/DZ EHC 122-34, M890-902.

DATE AND LOCATION: August, 1813-November, 1838, with gaps in 1816 and 1820-24. Clements Lane, Cockspur Street, London.

FORMAT: 12 volumes. The clasped oblong volumes are bound in brown leather and most contain blotter paper. The entries are written lengthwise with the month and date entered along the left-hand side of the page. The diarist draws lines to demarcate daily entry boundaries, and sometimes to separate events occurring on the same date. She occasionally marks months incorrectly. New volumes are a chronological continuation of previous volumes.

CONTENT: The diary volumes kept for the greater part of twenty-five years by the daughter of a Cockspur Street tradesman, later the wife of William Boycott, a businessman in the City, show how the social activities of a middle-class London girl are replaced by the duties and anxieties of marriage and motherhood. The earlier diary volumes detail the pursuits of the Holtzapfel family, and especially of Charlotte and her sister Caroline, who frequently attend the Covent Garden and Drury Lane theaters, Vauxhall, exhibitions at Somerset House, and charity sermons. The sisters often dance until early morning, and Charlotte uses her diary to list her partners as well as to mention events of the day, such as the illuminations celebrating victory at Waterloo, the procession of the Prince Regent and Louis XVIII, the coronation of Queen Victoria, and the Wallingford Hiring Fair. Charlotte also notes guests at supper, dinner, and tea, and describes her handiwork, which consists of caps, bodices, spencers, and dresses. Her sister Caroline's letters cover the period of Charlotte's missing journals; the former are also housed in the Wigan Record Office.

The missing diary volumes signal a change in Charlotte's life, for the later volumes show her attending lectures, marrying, worrying about her own and her husband's health, and having children. In the course of the entry describing her wedding, she signals her changed relationship with her husband by calling him for the first time by his Christian name. In the entries written during her honeymoon she describes her feelings of homesickness. Her accounts of childbirth are especially revealing, for she describes the process and its after-effects in detail, and indicates the extent to which women help each other through the ordeal. She is very concerned about her children's health and recounts her problems with feeding them and obtaining a wet nurse. Her father, mother-in-law, and two of her three children die; and the anguish caused by her second son's death from convulsions is aggravated by her own poor health and her husband's debilitated condition. Because of habitual illness in her family, Charlotte notes common medical remedies and practices. When the diary abruptly ends, her husband's symptoms of tuberculosis remain.

STYLISTIC FEATURES: The early entries are fragmentary, distanced, and terse and exhibit spelling errors and a lack of punctuation. Daily occurrences of little import to the diarist are jotted down without reaction, and occasionally she writes "nothing particular" beside a date. Her later entries are personal and detailed, especially when she chronicles momentous matters such as marriage, childbirth, and death. She suspends her diary-keeping when such events intervene and then writes summary entries to describe them. Later entries tend to be written in full sentences, although if the subject is the diarist the personal pronoun is often omitted.

PC4.

JOHNSTON, JANE (b. ?, d. 1840), Hertfordshire Record Office MS 16195-16217.

DATE AND LOCATION: 1817; 1819-40. Wimpole Street, London.

FORMAT: 23 volumes. The writer used several different

types of diaries with printed formats while writing her twenty-three volumes. The first kind combines the keeping of accounts with appointments and observations, so that the pocketbook volumes contain pages which are divided into spaces for monies received and paid as well as spaces for memoranda. The same dates serve to keep track of appointments, memoranda, and observations, which are located on the verso page, and to note expenditures, which are to be recorded on the recto page. The recto page is divided into vertical columns with designations for cash received and paid; these columns are subdivided into sections for pounds, shillings, and pence. The month and year are printed at the top of the pages. Volumes of this type may be designated as ledgers and are constructed of either leather or pasteboard. They contain useful information such as the listings of London bankers; hackney coach fares; clerks and officers of the House of Peers; births, marriages, and deaths of eminent people; and an abstract of the acts concerning coins, bank notes, and bank tokens. There are also pages for general accounts and memoranda which were not utilized by the diarist.

The second type of volume, which is usually made of pasteboard in varying hues, does not contain divisions for accounts. There are spaces for three entries on the verso page and four on the recto page with a smaller space for the Sunday entry. Useful information such as holidays at the bank or exchequer, as well as the month, the week of the month, and year, are printed at the top of the page. This type of volume also includes details of army and navy agents, law offices, hackney coach regulations, university terms, commercial stamps, and times of proceeding at the courts.

Yet a third type of diary is <u>The Student's Journal</u>, which is pasteboard with a mottled cover. The introduction to the journal explains its use, which is to keep track of each day's studies. Hence, the dates are to be inscribed by the student, and the space for Sunday is twice as large, since the diarist might read or reflect more on that day. The volume also contains an appendix where the student can remark about various books or evaluate a period of study, as well as an annual retrospect which encourages self-examination, although the editors point out that the volume is meant to inspire action, not speculation.

Jane Johnston, however, maintains this volume much as she does the other varieties, for she consistently uses her diaries to note accounts, social obligations, and events. She often employs the inside covers and the blank pages of her volumes to list miscellaneous information such as addresses, useful remedies, and the dates of leases or rents due. She often does not make entries while traveling; and she desires to preserve the accuracy of her account as she corrects mistaken entries. Occasionally she makes no prose entries; she constantly uses the page for accounts.

CONTENT: The widow of Henry George Johnston used her twenty-three volumes to keep track of engagements, letters received and sent, household and traveling expenditures, family and public events, servants' wages, amounts won or lost at cards, donations to charity, important deaths and births, her illnesses, and the weather. Her penchant for detailing the expenses of her daily life may arise from her position as a well-born lady living on a pension. Her record is an excellent source for the value of items and the services frequently used by a woman of her position, for Jane Johnston lists the costs of various household and personal articles such as coal, beer, sugar, lace, epsom salts, hair oil, hired carriages, washing, mahogany screens, silk stockings, paper, and chimney pots. She also notes payments to the chimney sweep, the day-laborer, the housemaid, and the painter. She mentions the marriage of her son Frederick and later the birth of his daughter, and records the deaths of George III and Princess Charlotte. Her diaries are employed as well to balance her accounts with her son, and describe his experiences, since both his living expenses and a notation of his amusements at the theater fall within the scope of her record.

STYLISTIC FEATURES: The short entries are written in sentence fragments and the diarist habitually lists expenses. Since she enters social engagements and the cost of items with no differentiation between the two, these categories seem to dovetail in the diarist's mind.

A number of entries merely record the weather. The entries are a bit longer when she describes country house visits.

PC5.
STEVENS, ELIZA HOPE, THE GOVERNESS OF (b. ?, d. ?), Hertfordshire Record Office MS 86326.
DATE AND LOCATION: October 1820-June 1821.
FORMAT: The small paper volume is inscribed on the inside front cover with the pupil's name (Eliza Hope Stevens) and the date. Initially, the daily entries are demarcated by a line drawn with a ruler to separate them; later they are separated by a space. Each week is dated, with the subsequent days of the week designated only by the day; in January 1821, however, some of the entries are not dated.
CONTENT: The behavior book of nine-year-old Eliza Hope Stevens, composed by her unnamed governess, illustrates the education in both manners and subject matter of a child in the last century and the role the governess played in this process. Eliza's attempt at learning almost always fell far short of the anticipated mark, and at the end of the account Eliza must wear the black ticket of disgrace for two days. Eliza's subjects are English and Roman history, French, grammar, poetry, arithmetic, geography, and Scripture. In addition, she is to be proficient at dancing, drawing, chronology, and mental improvement. Eliza is either indifferent or

careless about her studies, according to her governess's daily ratings of her progress. Her governess is particularly disturbed by Eliza's inattention in church, her lack of desire to learn, and her habitual disrespect towards others. The governess addresses Eliza when she records that she regrets having to censure her pupil, for she is certain Eliza will repent of her behavior as a child when she reads the volume as an adult. The governess refers several times to the goodness of Eliza's mother and indicates her own precarious position between mother and child when she says how sorry she is to distress Eliza's mother by recording her daughter's wrongdoing. The governess's personal frustration surfaces as well, for she writes how much Eliza's disrespectfulness toward her duty and her governess annoys her teacher.
STYLISTIC FEATURE: The length of the entries varies. If the governess simply rates Eliza's progress with the usual one-word evaluation of her pupil's lessons, the entries are relatively short. If, however, the governess comments more fully on Eliza's conduct, the entries are much longer. The latter are written in long, complex sentences which reveal the governess's position, particularly when the governess addresses questions to Eliza about her behavior, which the teacher then answers for her pupil.

PC6.
ANONYMOUS OF HULL (b. ?, d. ?), Wigan Record Office M864

EHC 96.

DATE AND LOCATION: January-September, 1833. Brighton; Clapham; London; Oxford; Cheltenham, Gloucestershire; Wales.

FORMAT: The bound half-crimson morocco volume contains daily entries demarcated by the date on the side of the page. The latter part of the diary originally contained sketches, now lost.

CONTENT: The diary kept by a young girl, who was perhaps a relative of the painter William Etty, records her activities during visits to friends and relatives in southern England and during a sketching tour in Wales. The first part of her account, which is maintained during her travels in England, describes typical activities such as attending church, dining out, settling accounts, and reading to others. She comments on the Sunday sermon and notes the verse and chapter discussed. When she attends a wedding, she writes that the ceremony was very interesting and painfully exciting. During her visit to London she goes to the House of Commons, the National Gallery, and Westminster Bridge, as well as to the grand bazaar and several dioramas. An account of the sketching tour, which follows the course of the Wye, forms the second part of the diary. Her sister Mary and her aunt and uncle accompanied the diarist on this sojourn, which featured touring estates, sketching churches, and contemplating the beauty and grandeur of nature.

STYLISTIC FEATURES: The punctuation is sporadic and

PROFESSIONAL-COMMERCIAL

there is little recording of the diarist's reactions. The entry length varies according to the amount of description sparked by the day's activities. Sometimes the diarist refers to herself as "I"; at other times she subsumes her identity in the collective "we". She frequently uses the adjective "sweet".

PC7.
LAPIDGE, MARIANNE (b. 1818, d. 1902), Wigan Record Office M841 EHC 72.
DATE AND LOCATION: 1833? Hampton Wick, London.
FORMAT: This volume, which cost two shillings and sixpence, is a <u>Marshall's Ladies Pocket Engagement Atlas for 1827</u>. It is made of full blue morocco with a tuck-in flap. It features facing color plates of a lady at a fair and a lady standing at a piano. The contents include catalogues of new music, new dances, the royal family, hackney coach fares, wage tables, London bankers, philosophical amusements, anecdotes, charades, enigmas, holidays, poetry, foreign monies, and public funds. There is a note to correspondents, which lists those whose charades and enigmas were accepted, as well as a notice of the publisher's contest being continued. The back of the volume has printed views of castles, which are accompanied by written descriptions, and advertisements by the publisher for family account books and ladies' pocket books.

 The entries, which apparently are for 1833, are very

irregularly maintained and are not confined to the spaces provided for them. The dates of the entries made by the diarist do not correspond to the printed dates, which are marked through with pencil. Most of the events related occurred between June 15 and July 15.

CONTENT: The diary, which was kept by the fifteen-year-old daughter of the architect Edward Lapidge, relates in particular the strained relationship between Marianne's ten-year-old sister, Fanny, and the girls' music master, Mr. Williams. Mr. Williams seems to have instructed the girls largely through insulting them. When their playing or singing was bad, he told them that they ate too much for dinner, that their curls were too profuse over their ears, or that they were just like schoolgirls, his favorite insult since, as Marianne observes, he seems to have held schoolgirls in great contempt. The diarist records at which points the girls' mother was present during a conversation where Mr. Williams told Fanny she deserved to be flogged for her inept playing. Marianne does not, however, give her mother's reactions to Mr. Williams's assertions. She mentions when Fanny was rude to Mr. Williams.

STYLISTIC FEATURES: Many of the entries are only one or two words, and in some instances the pencil entries have been almost totally erased or crossed through. The entries between the middle of June and the middle of July are written in very descriptive dialogue. When the diarist refers to herself she usually employs the third person and spells the name "Marian".

PC8.

DICKENSON, ELIZA (b. 1818, d. ?), Gloucestershire Record Office MSS. D36 F33-41.

DATE AND LOCATION: July, 1836-June, 1846, with gaps each year from 1840-46. Volume 4, which covers August, 1837 to January, 1838, is missing. Bombay, Poona, India; The Wilderness, Mitcheldean, Gloucestershire.

FORMAT: Nine volumes. Although the volumes are of varying sizes, all are made of pressed paper and have brown corners and spines. Most of the volumes are marked by the diarist's name, the date, and the location, although the seventh volume is not inscribed and some of the later volumes do not show the diarist's name. Volume three in particular contains erasures and razored-out pages, although these characteristics are common to all the volumes. Volumes five to nine have summary entries and pages left blank by the diarist. Inside volume seven there is a sheaf of stationery which is stitched together to construct a journal in which the diarist describes an expedition with her husband. The entries are kept daily initially but become more sporadic after the diarist's marriage.

CONTENT: Eliza Dickenson, the daughter of Colonel Thomas Dickenson, an Army chief engineer in Bombay, and later the wife of Francis Wemyss, a major in the Bombay Engineers, started her diary in response to her brother

Tom's death from cholera. The first two volumes of her record help her cope with this loss. She writes her diary partly as a tribute to Tom, since through its construction she attempts to follow his example by admonishing herself to do as he would have done. Keeping a diary enables Eliza to reconcile herself to change and uncertainty, which are symbolized for her by the harsh reality of death, but which she strives to view as part of God's plan. Her diary also records the grieving process undergone by a Victorian family. The family consoles itself by reading aloud sermons, memoirs, and most importantly Tom's journals. Eliza's role in the familial grieving process is significant, since her father requests that she transcribe Tom's journals, and since she habitually comforts her mother over the death of her son.

Eliza considers reading diaries a very important activity because journals reveal feeling, a trait she thinks most men lack. She is extremely critical of men as a class. According to Eliza, men have power only because they deny women knowledge. She condemns fictional presentations of women where the change in the heroine's character is not accounted for, since this undermines women's already inferior position. She objects to women being described as angelic and then characterized as unnatural. The relationship between the sexes forms a principal theme in her early volumes, but after she marries in 1838 she makes few comments about men. She considers marriage a loss of self analogous to death and dreads sexual contact with her husband. She also fears marriage because it means separation from her sister, Fanny, upon whom she relied for emotional support.

After Eliza's marriage her entries primarily report daily activities such as laundering her husband's clothes, keeping accounts, and writing letters. Frank's protracted absence during the early years of their marriage causes Eliza much anxiety, just as does the marriage of her sister. Both events make Eliza fear she will lose loved ones. She records the trials occasioned by the birth of her children in 1842 and 1843 as well as the support derived from the exchange of secret notes between herself and her sister who is also pregnant. Re-reading her journal in 1844 causes Eliza to upbraid herself for her slackness as a diary writer, since she believes writing her journal develops well-directed thinking and enables others to see the main springs of character; hence, she again begins to summarize her readings, a staple of her earlier journals. She discontinues this, however, when her husband's sickness forces a return to England, and her volume ends in 1846 with a description of Frank's illness, which he contracted in India. He died in 1848.

STYLISTIC FEATURES: The early entries are quite long. The convoluted sentence structures, which often lack sufficient punctuation, indicate the diarist's introspective and questioning mind. She typically composes her early entries by relating a specific incident and then giving her reaction to it. Her language is rather distanced and moralistic when she marries and consequently must part with her family. Erasures and the razoring out of pages occur when highly personal events take place. The diarist describes childbirth in summary entries, and her handwriting is more illegible in later volumes. The entries become shorter after 1837 and very brief between 1842 and 1844. There are summary entries during and after 1840.

PC9.
MENCE, SARAH (b. ?, d. ?), Wigan Record Office M812 EHC 144.
DATE AND LOCATION: February, 1840.
FORMAT: There is one entry written on the endpaper and inside cover of Richard Mangnall's <u>Historical</u> <u>and</u> <u>Miscellaneous</u> <u>Questions</u> <u>for</u> <u>the</u> <u>Use</u> <u>of</u> <u>Young</u> <u>People</u>.
CONTENT: This single entry, composed by a schoolgirl on the day Queen Victoria was married to Prince Albert, begins with the diarist wondering if the Queen is enjoying her day. The diarist, who is not enjoying hers, proceeds to wish for oranges and to speculate about her sister's homecoming. She comments on the weather and her feelings of desolation, claiming that she wrote this entry to amuse herself later. She concludes by saying that she deserves to be scolded for not knowing her lessons.
STYLISTIC FEATURES: This brief personal entry expresses the diarist's wants, and indicates by its inclusion on a

book's inside cover, the immediacy of the diarist's drive for self-expression.

PC10.
COATES, ELIZA (b. ?, d. ?), Gloucestershire Record Office D3980/1.
DATE AND LOCATION: 1846, 1848. London; Cheltenham, Gloucestershire.
FORMAT: The leather-covered volume contains about thirty pages, which are ruled for an account book. On the inside front cover there is a stamp table. The volume is inscribed with the date and the diarist's name. The 1848 entries directly follow those for 1846.
CONTENT: This diary was apparently kept by a young woman from Monmouth to record events during her travels; the 1846 entries detail her sojourn in London, while the 1848 entries characterize her stay at Cheltenham. Her stay in London is dominated by the figure of Henry, presumably her fiancé. Virtually every entry mentions his whereabouts and her feelings towards him. She also describes visiting London sights such as the Royal Exchange, the British Museum, and the Pantheon; shopping in Oxford and High Streets; and seeing a performance of The Merry Wives of Windsor.

The 1848 segment of the diary is a brief account of a family argument about the expense and inconvenience of travelling to Cheltenham.
STYLISTIC FEATURES: The entries are brief but inclusive,

since the diarist gives her reactions to events in detail.

PC11.

HUMPHREYS, ELIZABETH (b. 1806, d. 1863), National Library of Wales, Glousevern 14, 743.

DATE AND LOCATION: January-March, probably 1847. London.

FORMAT: The volume has marbled pasteboard covers with green binding and corner tips. Only about one-third of the diary is filled with entries, which begin with the date and sometimes the day. At the back of the volume when inverted are several poems copied in the diarist's hand, including Wordsworth's Intimations Ode.

CONTENT: Although this diary is catalogued by the National Library of Wales as that of a single woman, it is obvious from its content that the writer is a married woman whose husband is a barrister often engaged in dealing with inventions. The diarist mentions her fifteen-month-old child and problems with servants, though one of her principal occupations is performing secretarial work for her husband. She is preoccupied with running the household smoothly and hence is frustrated when the breakfast dishes are not cleared away before nine o'clock. She details her dental problems, her reading, and the severe weather.

The most interesting aspect of her diary is its commentary on the relationship between the sexes. She recounts an argument about the differences between clubs and homes and the pleasures of married men versus those of bachelors. She also narrates a tale told by a doctor about a young woman who died because she was insufficiently clothed. The moral drawn by the doctor was that bad health often occurred because of a person's neglect of duty and virtue.

STYLISTIC FEATURES: Her journal is written in terse language which characterizes the diarist's determined outlook. The entries are composed in elliptical fragments; for example, when she refers to a guest remaining in bed she omits the verb.

PC12.
MIERS, MRS. S. M. (b. ?, d. ?), Wigan Record Office M795 EHC 27.
DATE AND LOCATION: July, 1850-June, 1860, with some gaps. London; Birmingham; Rio de Janerio, Brazil.
FORMAT: The thick volume bound in dark red morocco had clasps which have been removed. There are marbled inner covers and the pages are ruled down the left margin. The entries, which usually run four to a page, are generally daily. There are gaps in the entries when the diarist is ill from childbirth or is nursing relatives, friends, and children; when she returns to Brazil from England; or occasionally when she takes short trips.
CONTENT: The diary maintained by the wife of Francis Charles Miers, a shipbuilder in Rio de Janerio, begins

with the diarist's account of her departure from England for Brazil where she lived as a child. She keenly regrets leaving her family in England and consequently undergoes insomnia before the voyage, a reaction which often occurs during her stressful or exciting experiences. She catalogues the other passengers on board the ship, as well as her own activities, which include reading, reciting poetry, drawing, playing chess, singing, and learning Portuguese. Her fiancé meets her in Rio de Janerio, and the entries which follow detail the preparations for her marriage to "Frank." She relies on her sister-in-law Caroline for emotional and physical assistance before the marriage, which entails a civil ceremony conducted at the British Consulate and a church wedding. The church wedding is less trying than she feared, although she regrets her parents' absence, particularly her dead father's. At the end of the entry which describes the church wedding, she tries on her new identity by inscribing her married name. Shortly after her honeymoon she first experiences morning sickness, a condition which features regularly in her diary, since she bore five children in the ten years covered by her account.

Her journal indicates the extent to which the English transplanted their culture. Her daily activities during the first part of her diary include numerous visits to friends and relatives, problems with servants, and a lot of reading. She peruses all the major writers of the period, including Carlyle, De Quincey, Tennyson, Thackeray, Dickens, Hawthorne, Poe, Byron, Goethe, Charlotte Brontë, and Macaulay. She also reads her sister's travel diaries and keeps a journal of her own activities for her mother. She consistently observes such anniversaries as New Year's, her mother's and sister's birthdays, and her father's death. She also writes accounts of her own and her husband's birthdays, and later of the anniversaries of their engagement and wedding. Little mention is made of her husband's business activities, other than remarks about his arrival or departure from home. Weather conditions often prevent her from leaving home, although she does participate in a round of social activities such as balls and the opera.

In July 1853 Mrs. Miers and her family return to England where they visit relatives and the sights of London. She goes to the Crystal Palace, the British Museum, a cattle show in Birmingham, and the Drury Lane Theater. Certainly the high point of her activities is attending a reading by Dickens of <u>The Cricket on the Hearth</u>. During her sojourn in England her grandfather suddenly dies and her nephew nearly does too. When she returns to Brazil her life resumes its former course, except that her concern with illness and childbirth increases.

Her first child, a boy, is born in August of 1851, and after this birth and each subsequent one, she describes both childbirth and her recovery from it. Her entries hint of her sensations during pregnancy, but it is the ritual of parturition which figures prominently in her account, for she remarks about the childbirths experienced by other women as well. She helps with these, particularly if they are difficult. When her sister-in-law Ellen becomes ill after the delivery of twins, Mrs. Miers nurses her and cares for Ellen's children. Mrs. Miers's account shows the significant role childbirth and illness played in the lives of Victorian women, for her diary also records incidents of cholera and dental problems. The diarist has at least eleven teeth extracted during the decade covered by her record, and the latter part of her diary is largely a recounting of illnesses suffered by her family or herself. She nearly dies after the birth of her fifth child. When Mrs. Miers is not sick or nursing others, she gives her children lessons, makes arrangements for their entertainments, or takes them to visit friends. Her diary is an excellent account of the duties and anxieties of Victorian motherhood.

STYLISTIC FEATURES: Generally the entries are about four sentences in length. The longest and most heartfelt entries are summaries which are written after the diarist's experiences with childbirth or illness, either her own or relatives. Before the birth of her children the diarist's entries become shorter, scrawled, and more illegible than usual. In the latter part of her record she begins to refer to herself and her children as "we" and to her husband as "dear Papa." When she describes her initial meeting with Frank just before their wedding, her diction is reminiscent of Thackeray and Dickens in its mood, insight, and narrative formality. Although her entries cover each day's activities, they are not necessarily recorded every day, as her striking of information entered under the inappropriate date signifies.

PC13.
ANONYMOUS OF BUCKINGHAMSHIRE (b. ?, d. ?), Wigan Record Office M923 EHC 138.
DATE AND LOCATION: 1852. Near Uxbridge, Buckinghamshire.
FORMAT: The black leather-bound volume has a strap which closes it and a paper pouch for memoranda. This Punch's Pocket-Book for 1852 features a four-page color fold-out entitled "Progress of Bloomerism; or a Complete Change." The scene depicts a parlor where men do the traditional work of women. The husband, who is holding the baby, asks his wife if she will dine at home today, and she replies that she will go to the club and to Greenwich to dine with the girls.

The pocket-book also contains memoranda and ruled pages for cash accounts for every day of the year, as well as lists of royalty, officers of the City, directors of the East India Company, and army agents. There are also significant dates for the courts, the theater, exhibitions, museums, and public offices, and tables of assessed taxes, hackney coach fares, and marketing. A week is displayed per page with notations of Christian dates and Sunday verses. At the end of the volume there is a printed section of stories, dramas, and farcical essays, all composed in the Punch style.

CONTENT: The diarist, who seems to have been a farmer's wife, used her printed volume largely as an account book. In the cash accounts section she lists daily receipts and expenditures for each month. In the pages of the diary she notes the receipt of letters, washing days, the purchase of sheep, and frequent trips to Uxbridge.

STYLISTIC FEATURES: The notations in the cash accounts section are very sketchy and illegible. The comments are brief and fragmentary.

PC14.

LEGGATT, FREDERICA CONSTANCE (b. 1843, d. 1928), Wigan Record Office M968 EHC 176.

DATE AND LOCATION: 1862-64; 1867. Knightsbridge, London; Brighton; Ewell, Surrey; Scotland.

FORMAT: Three volumes. The first two volumes are covered with blue embossed cloth; the third has a cover embossed in red; and all the volumes contain ruled sheets. The first two volumes include a single entry for October 1862, and daily entries with some gaps between March, 1863, and July, 1864. The third volume of 1867 features daily entries made during a tour of Scotland. Her entries are differentiated by the day and date, and there are illustrations which depict the diarist and members of her family. At the end of the third volume there is a fascinating tale entitled "The Parting for India," which describes through the voice of a male narrator the marriage and departure for India of his sister.

CONTENT: The first two diary volumes, which were kept by the unmarried daughter of a London doctor residing in Lowndes Square, London, picture her daily life in London and Brighton and at the home of her sister Marion in Ewell. One of twelve children, the diarist participates in the ordinary round of activities deemed proper for a young lady. Her first volume begins with a single entry for 1862, made the final day of the family's outing at the Great Exhibition. Croquet matches function as primary social events for the diarist, as does the Harvest Home fete. The lengthy account of the fete in her first volume indicates the class distinctions integral to the amusement's differing activities. She notes her grandfather's death, the birth of her sister's son, the illuminations to celebrate the Queen's birthday, the variety of games she played, and her joy when her parents rent a house at Brighton. She also uses her diary to record her readings, her nursing of relatives, her visits to the sick, her French, German, and music lessons, her teaching activities at a parish school, and her social engagements. Sometimes she registers the Bible verse and theme of the sermons she attends. Her reading included <u>Queen Mab</u>, <u>The Gladiators</u>, <u>The Idylls of the King</u>, and a variety of Dickens's novels.

She frequently reads aloud to others, especially the sick, and her relationship with the invalid women she visits is an important part of her record. One of the most significant passages in the second volume indicates the close relationship between the invalid and the woman who visits her, for the diarist is quite shocked when her friendship with a terminally ill woman is sundered by death. Another central part of Frederica's life involves teaching the parish children. She often comments about the success of the class and indicates whether she was sufficiently prepared. One of her principal entertainments is attending public readings. She regularly helps her father with his business. One lecture which she thought was excellent was about the nature of man, and included some men from the factory as exhibits. Her long entry about the celebration of her twenty-first birthday shows how much she enjoyed receiving presents and congratulations from a large gathering, even though she was disappointed her father's work kept him from attending. Her record illustrates the role of the Victorian patriarch, for she had to secure her father's permission before she could sing in a concert. She records her reaction to engagements and weddings. Her family's comments to her about her preference for widowers shows her interest in marriage.

The third volume records her journey to Scotland with her father and her sister Amy. The threesome visits Edinburgh, Glasgow, and Sir Walter Scott's home at

Abbotsford. The diarist also describes family events, since she remarks that her sister Gertrude is very devoted to her new baby. The tale, "The Parting for India," is located at the end of the third volume, and is written in the diarist's hand. It focuses on a woman's sacrifice for her husband, and it may obliquely refer to Frederica's sister Gertrude, who went with her husband to India where she bore four children and died.
STYLISTIC FEATURES: Her entries often begin by noting the birthday of one of the parish children she teaches. The entry length varies depending on the extent of her reaction to events, though ordinarily her Sunday entries are shorter. She sometimes omits the subject of the sentence, especially if it is herself, though usually she writes in complete sentences of medium length. There is enough detail to present clearly her reactions and the significance of events.

PC15.
SIMPSON, L. M. (b. 1839, d. ?), Wigan Record Office M822 EHC 53.
DATE AND LOCATION: July, 1878-July, 1880. Rutland Square, Dublin; Ireland; Scotland; southern and western England.
FORMAT: The black, cardboard pocket book volume contains ruled pages and daily entries, except initially where there is a gap between July and October. An inside front page is inscribed with the diarist's name and the date.

The entries are labeled by the day and the date.

CONTENT: This volume maintained by a widowed lady who stays with various relatives and friends pictures the unhappy life of a superfluous woman. She uses her diary to cope with an existence she found wretched, and much of her record depicts her conflicts with her Aunt Maria, an elderly lady living in Dublin with her nephew Coly, and frequently with the diarist. Mrs. Simpson blames herself for her dislike of her Aunt Maria, who forbids Mrs. Simpson to read novels on Saturday, and for the boredom she experiences while living with her aunt. In an effort to contend with her lot she asks God for help. She seems convinced that the solution to her isolation would be a home of her own, and accordingly, she obliquely wishes that a gentleman she meets would ask her to marry him. Because of her frustrations with her present situation, she frequently reminisces about the past and hopes for a better future. She notes her birthday and her mother's, as well as the anniversary of her wedding; and she poignantly recounts her visit to her parents' graves. Both her final entry of the year and the last entry in her diary express the desire for increased happiness in the future. When she is especially depressed she asks for death to release her from her monotonous existence.

Many of her entries record the names of her correspondents, since she is dependent upon others, and whether she has received invitations from them. Her visits of necessity to friends and relatives take her to the Isle of Wight, Southampton, Brighton, Cheltenham, and London, as well as to Glasgow, Cork, Killarney, Belfast, and Edinburgh. When a relative commits her to a holiday in France, she is anxious lest her income from investments, which is her source of revenue, becomes too depleted. When she is in Southampton she visits Lucy, who is apparently her late husband's illegitimate daughter. She writes critically of Lucy, as she does of many of the people she visits, for she very much resents her dependence on others; and she is particularly aggravated by her relatives' insistence that she nurse elderly family members. The latter part of her diary narrates her stay with her dying uncle Philip, whose senility she finds disgusting. Her principal relief during her stay with Uncle Philip derives from the company of her cousins, Nugent and Philip, Jr. She smokes with cousin Phil, often plays billiards, walks the dogs, and meets Nugent in London, where she frequently attends the theater. Uncle Philip dies during her residence with him, and she notes with disgust the custom of placing the coffin shell in the dining room. Her diary notes her ordinary activities, which include walking, reading, attending the theater and lectures, and taking drives. She also describes the pursuits of the people she visits, so that her record depicts the life of middle-class Victorians and shows as well the tensions inherent in their families. Her final entry indicates that she planned to continue keeping a diary.

STYLISTIC FEATURES: Her entries are longer if she experiences more family conflicts or if she participates in more activities. If she feels her existence is wretched, the entries are very short. She begins her entries by noting the weather, and then narrates the day's activities in order. Her highly distinctive diction contains several expressions for boredom or unhappiness, such as "dead slow," "very piano," and the "old treadmill life." Although she is not religious, she labels days according to their religious association.

PC16.

WILLIAMS, SARAH (b. ?, d. ?), National Library of Wales, Add. MS. 16760C.

DATE AND LOCATION: 1885; June, 1890-December, 1897. Llanbrynmain, Powys, Wales.

FORMAT: The black leather-covered volume has "Judge's Minute Book" embossed on the front and is inscribed with the diarist's name and "June 1885". There are red marbled paper inside front and rear covers, and the blue pages of the diary are ruled for accounts.

CONTENT: The volume, which is a combination account book and diary about bees, was kept by an unmarried woman whose business card describes her as a grocer, stationer, and dealer in china and fancy goods. In the 1885 segment about bees, the entries catalogue each hive and the origin of each swarm and estimate the profit made on the honey. The daily accounts, which run from 1890 to 1897, show the inventory for her store. She notes the weather and the arrival of such goods as tea, sugar, cheese, flour, coal, beef, brandy, and china. There are also some personal entries which primarily list deaths. She records loans and their repayment, as well as calvings, lambings, and hirings. Her extensive accounts indicate that she was a woman well-versed in financial and managerial responsibilities.

STYLISTIC FEATURES: The brief entries are written in English and Welsh and show by their terseness the simple equating of personal and financial matters. The entries in Welsh become more frequent later.

PC17.
VEREY, MISS I. E. (b. ?, d. ?), Wigan Record Office M792 EHC 24.
DATE AND LOCATION: September, 1889. Shrewsbury to Streatley, Berkshire.
FORMAT: The bound leather volume is engraved on the front in gilt with "Shrewsbury to Streatley." The title page contains a sketch of a boat and the inscription "Recollections of a boating tour down the Severn from Shrewsbury to Gloucester, thro' the Berkeley Canal 'Stroud Water,' 'Thames & Severn' Canals, the Golden Valley of Stroud, Sapperton Tunnel, & into the Upper Thames & on past Oxford & Abingdon to Streatley--1889." There are daily entries for the first several days; later

the entries are composed retrospectively.

CONTENT: The travel diary kept by an unmarried young woman, who resided at Childe Court, Streatley, Reading, records her journey by canal between September 3rd and 20th, 1889. The first entry is a poem about commencing the journey written by the diarist. Her travelogue recounts the sights viewed by the group, who traversed approximately one hundred miles in a randan. The diarist notes the condition of the canals and the randan's dimensions, as well as its transportation by rail or steamer when the group is not rowing the randan. Pen-and-ink sketches of mediocre merit and photographs purchased en route illustrate the canal tour. The diarist describes the weather, the lodgings, and the food, and underlines noteworthy sights such as the Malvern Hills, Oxford, or the picturesque village of Arley. The diarist ends her account by saying that if you are tempted to follow the same route she hopes you will enjoy the journey as much as her group did.

STYLISTIC FEATURES: The use of the collective pronoun "we" throughout the diary and the author's closing remark signal its function as a travelogue which was meant to be read by others. This use is also supported by the collection of sketches, photographs, and letters about the trip contained in the diary, and by the diarist's habit of underlining places of interest. Much of the diary was apparently written after the journey.

PC18.

WILLIAMS, ELEANOR (b. ?, d. ?), National Library of Wales, Add. MS. 2683.

DATE AND LOCATION: 1890. Wales.

FORMAT: The purple pasteboard volume has a front cover engraved in gilt with the inscription "Collins' Portable Diary 1890." Hand inscribed by the diarist, the volume includes information typical for this period; for instance, there are advertisements for other diaries and reckoners, a calendar for 1890, and catalogues of postal rates, servants' wages, and tables of interest. The volume has four spaces per page with the last recto space designated as a weekly summary. At the end of the diary there are pages for memoranda, an annual cash summary, and advertisements for atlases and dictionaries.

CONTENT: This printed diary kept by a Welsh woman, who appears to be a farmer's wife, contains entries about the weather and farm activities. The diarist notes if the weather is fine or wet, what animals were sold at the fair and for what price, and the harvesting of crops. She also lists family and community deaths.

STYLISTIC FEATURES: The brief entries are characterized by inaccurate spelling and grammar; for example, she spells "here" without the second e, uses improper verb-subject agreement, and confuses the subjective and objective pronoun cases.

PC19.

LARMUTH, HELENA (b. 1875, d. ?), Wigan Record Office M1239 EHC 219.

DATE AND LOCATION: March, 1891-May, 1892. Handforth, near Manchester, Cheshire.

FORMAT: A one-volume typescript edited by Edward Hall is all that remains of the original diary. The editor has selected many daily entries for inclusion in the typescript.

CONTENT: The diary of the daughter of a Manchester businessman, G. H. Larmuth, is an excellent account of the restrictions faced by a sixteen-year-old who used her writing to help her cope with her familial situation. Nelly, as she calls herself, is continually forced to remain at home because she is the only girl. Composing her diary helps her escape such confinement by allowing Nelly to control a part of her world.

Nelly's record acutely depicts her longing to have been born a male. One way she gains some of the freedom she associates with being male is by riding horses; and her wish to perfect her skill as a rider forms a principal theme in her diary. An even more important ambition for Nelly is becoming an author. Her ability as a diarist shows that she achieved her desire, for Nelly's account perceptively assesses her own behavior and that of others. Like many nineteenth-century women diarists, Nelly used her diary to evaluate her behavior. She consistently found herself unable to behave as was expected of her. Nelly's failure to conform to the Victorian standard of feminine behavior placed her at odds with her mother in particular. Her father chided Nelly for her actions as well, though she loved him dearly. Nelly was fond of her brothers too, and their return from school gave her some of the companionship which ordinarily only her diary supplied.

A highly significant event in Nelly's diary is her trip to the Isle of Man, since this allowed her to escape the confinement of housework. Consequently, her sojourn there functions as a primary structural feature of the diary. Nelly relives her stay on the Isle of Man by re-reading her entries; as she indicates in her final entry, one excellent reason for keeping a diary is that this allows the writer to experience the past again.
STYLISTIC FEATURES: The entry length depends on the amount the diarist has to relate, but usually the entries are long and detailed. The sentence length varies. Often the diary itself is directly addressed. The diarist perceptively depicts her situation through the use of well-chosen words. There are some mistakes in spelling.

PC20.
RAMSDEN, DIANA (b. ?, d. ?), Wigan Record Office M787 EHC 119.
DATE AND LOCATION: November, 1899-September, 1900, with gaps. Queensland, Australia.
FORMAT: The rebound cloth volume contains a typescript

written by the diarist and entitled by her, "Beautiful Queensland and Leaves From My Diary." The volume includes watercolor illustrations by the diarist of Australian scenes, plants, and animal life. There are daily entries initially with many gaps later, particularly from the end of December to March and from the end of March to July.

CONTENT: The typescript, edited from her original diary by an intelligent and educated Englishwoman who visits friends in Queensland, sets out to contradict her former impressions of life in the Australian bush. As she writes near the beginning of her account, her diary will relate what she actually experienced. Both her illustrations and her prose depict the quiet beauty and ruggedness of Australian bush life. She emphasizes the absence of boredom for ladies living in Queensland, for in contrast to English ladies, they frequently have to do the work of housemaids and cooks, put out a bush fire, or muster cattle. They perform such tasks cheerfully, always remain hospitable, and are more contented than many Englishwomen who experience far fewer trials.

The diarist points out there are many interesting activities for a lady to pursue in the bush, such as sewing, painting, writing letters, and listening to music; and in fact she implicitly recommends immigration for gentlewomen. She believes many redundant Englishwomen would be happier acting as the companion for a lonely woman in the bush than teaching in England. She indicates how fond the colonials are of reading novels and the English illustrated papers, which they obtain from circulating libraries and reading rooms. Although she admits that Australian girls are very hospitable, she criticizes them as self-satisfied, forward, and incompletely educated, since their interests center on riding and novel reading. An especially good indication of the rugged life encountered at a Queensland station is the vivid description of the killing of a snake by one of her host's several fox terriers. She also makes some acute observations about the disappearance of the aborigines.

STYLISTIC FEATURES: The long, vivid personal descriptions are accompanied by pictorial illustrations. The diarist does not write a travelogue, but an account of her impressions and experiences, which contrast with British notions of Queensland.

I1.
GALTON, EMMA (b. 1812, d. 1904), University College Library, London, Galton Papers, Item 37. See also Galton, Louisa.
DATE AND LOCATION: 1829-98, with gaps. Leamington.
FORMAT: The volume is a typescript of annual entries, which are arranged not chronologically but associationally, both by the diarist and the typist. The numbers of the manuscript pages are listed before the entries by the typist. The dates of journeys are separated from

other significant yearly dates. The deaths and marriages which occur in a given year may be listed either at the beginning or the ending of the entry for that year; eventually Emma Galton subsumes these and similar events under the category of "life changes." The diarist corrects some entry listings, so that the proper events are entered for the appropriate year. Additional entries for 1829-47 appear at the end of the typescript.

CONTENT: The unmarried daughter of Samuel T. Galton, a Birmingham banker, and the sister of the eugenicist Francis Galton, Emma maintained the family record previously kept by her sister Elizabeth. Her retrospective account concentrates on significant family events, such as the death of her father in 1844 and the subsequent dissolution of the family home. As the chronicler of family activities, Emma includes the noteworthy achievements of her brothers, and her relatives' engagements, marriages, and deaths. She notes unusual changes in others' lives, such as May Galton's conversion to Catholicism. Family illnesses form part of her record, as does the computation of family finances. The diary evidences some of Emma's personal concerns, such as the publication of The Unprotected, her book of financial advice for unmarried women, her journeys and the new places she visits, her arrangements with her maid, and her position as secretary at a cooking school. Some public events are included, such as the Crystal Palace Exhibition and the death of King William IV. At the end of her record Emma cites memorabilia. Several of these final memorable entries concern Louisa's bequests to Emma and indicate the close relationship between the two women. The final item is a rather derogatory poem, persumably about the diarist, which was composed by her father.

STYLISTIC FEATURES: The cryptic, fragmentary entries are arranged associationally. She refers to herself in the first person and her comments about family activities are slightly more detailed than the listings about her travels.

I2.
GALTON, LOUISA (b. 1822, d. 1896), University College Library, London, Galton Papers, Items 53, 55. See also Galton, Emma.

DATE AND LOCATION: 1830-96. Rutland Gate, London.

FORMAT: Two volumes. The first volume of the Annual Record is entered in a black bound notebook which begins with a biographical sketch by his mother of the first eight years of Francis Galton's life. At the time of her marriage to Francis in 1853, Louisa Galton commenced keeping the record, but she prefaced it with an account of the years 1830-53. Her retrospective survey begins in 1830, the year Mrs. Galton's sketch ends. It includes only brief details for 1830-34, but from 1834 until their marriage Louisa writes slightly longer accounts of her own and her husband's lives on separate pages, labeling one "Frank's Life," the other "Louisa's Life."

When the couple is married, Louisa joins the accounts, although between 1854-57 the joint accounts are not written on Frank's verso page, but on hers. Beginning in 1858 she uses both the recto and verso pages.

The second volume is octavo and bound in red cloth with lined blue pages, and contains on the inside front cover in Louisa's hand, "A Continuation of Our Yearly Summary." Louisa enters the date of the current year in the volume, followed by a description of the principal events of the preceding year.

CONTENT: The diaries are ostensibly a family record kept by Louisa Galton, the daughter of a former headmaster of Harrow and Dean of Peterborough, and wife of the eugenicist and scientist, Francis Galton. The early entries give brief details of the childhood family activities of Louisa and Francis, mentioning such matters as illnesses, schooling, and social debut. The entries written during their marriage mention Francis Galton's scientific achievements; public and political occurrences such as the invention of the telephone, Gordon's mission to Khartoum, and Gladstone's political defeat; and the significant events for siblings and other family members and friends, including births, deaths, marriages, and achievements.

Louisa's recording of her reactions to family events, such as her remark after the deaths of her own and Francis's mother that now both houses are gone, indicates the diary's status as a family record. But Louisa also uses her account to maintain and strengthen her own identity, and consequently writes of the importance of her relationship with Francis's sister Emma, her sojourns on the Continent, her habitual problems with servants, her chronic illness, and her forebodings of death. Especially in the second volume, Louisa views others in relation to herself and her declining health. Louisa's use of poetic descriptions, which presage death and symbolize the inevitable decay of all things, helps free her from the confinement resulting from ill health and her role as the family chronicler.

STYLISTIC FEATURES: The early entries are short and are often written in fragments. In some of the entries referring to Francis, Louisa calls him by his Christian name; at other times she assumes his voice and writes "I;" and sometimes she deletes the pronoun. The latter entries contain poetic descriptions, such as her personification of the fog, and are quite long, often running about five pages, even though Louisa protests that she has nothing to say. These tend to follow a pattern which begins with a summary of her illnesses, remarks about the couple's holidays on the Continent, and descriptions of family activities. This is followed by comments about Francis Galton's scientific achievements and noteworthy political events.

T3.
WARD, MARY AUGUSTA (b. 1851, d. 1920), University College

Library, London, MS. Add. 202, Item 2. See also Ward, Dorothy.

DATE AND LOCATION: 1885-87; 1892-98. "Stocks," Aldbury, Hertfordshire; London; Vienna; Paris; Ireland.

FORMAT: 10 volumes. Eight of the ten volumes are editions of Smith's Small Scribbling Diary, which is bound in brown cloth with the year embossed on the cover. There is an almanac of the year at the beginning of the volume followed by useful information about stamp duties, London cab fares, the royal family, the post office, and principal governmental officers and bankers. The listings under assessed taxes indicate the duties on dogs, armorial bearings, carriages, male servants, and houses. Memoranda pages proceed the section for entries which has spaces on each page for three entries. Above the entries are printed Bible lessons and noteworthy information, such as when the Fire Insurance expires or when the terms at Oxford and Cambridge begin. The Victorian desire to order time is reflected in the publisher's citation of the month, the year, the weeks of the year, the day and date, and the number of days in the year which have passed and which are to come. This information is located at the top of each page. There is blotter paper between the pages.

The 1893 volume is an Army and Navy Octavo Scribbling Diary, and the 1898 volume is a Pettitt's Octavo Diary. Both of these kinds of diaries contain information similar to that in Smith's though both have more advertisements than do the Smith's versions. Interestingly, these printed volumes often advertise other types of diaries, such as The Housekeeper's Diary, the Lady's Washing Book, and the Office Desk Diary. The Army and Navy volume has spaces for three entries on the verso page and four entries on the recto page, while the Pettitt's provides two entries per page. All ten volumes were sporadically kept by the diarist.

CONTENT: The family diaries, which were maintained by the novelist Mary Ward in conjunction with her husband Humphrey, list social activities such as dinner engagements, garden parties, fancy dress balls, and attendance at the theater. The notations of dinner guests feature members of the English intelligentsia including the Thomas Huxleys and Matthew Arnold. Humphrey Ward mentions political events, like the division on the Home Rule Bill, much more frequently than does Mary, who notes the blooming of flowers and the produce of plants. The volumes were employed to keep track of the children's activities, family theatricals, and significant events in London and the nation, such as the death of Gladstone. In the 1893 and 1894 volumes newspaper clippings citing the excessive heat and cold are pasted in. Beginning in 1892 Mary starts to take over the maintenance of the family diary so that more of the entries concern her interests. For example, she dates her public readings and the completion of her novels as well as her charitable work. The volumes are also used to chronicle the

journeys of family members to Paris, Ireland, and Vienna.
STYLISTIC FEATURES: There are brief remarks which merely outline the activities of family members. The descriptions of journeys are slightly more detailed, though even when the spaces allowed for entries are larger they do not contain more remarks. The diarists do not refer to themselves by the personal pronoun, but instead by their initial or by their Christian name. In later volumes Mary refers to herself and her husband as "Mrs." and "Mr." She also calls herself "Mother."

I4.
WARD, DOROTHY MARY (b. 1874, d. 1960), University College Library, London, MSS. Add. 202. See also Ward, Mary Augusta.
DATE AND LOCATION: 1890 and 1898. Grosvenor Place, London; "Stocks," Aldbury, Hertfordshire; Ireland; Paris; Italy.
FORMAT: Two volumes. The two pocket volumes are a Walker's Diary and a Charles Letts's Improved Pocket Diary. On the outside of the packet containing the 1890 Walker's volume is an inscription noting that Dorothy's diary was a present from her uncle William. The Walker's volume begins with a calendar, which is followed by several pages lined for daily appointments with the appropriate date and day running down the left-hand side of the page. Some of the lines for appointments are utilized by the diarist but after February she omits this

practice. In the Walker's volume there are spaces for four daily entries on the verso page and spaces for three daily entries, plus one for memoranda, on the recto page. The 1898 Letts's diary features a page for each daily entry and at the beginning of the volume includes a calendar as well as pages for engagements, addresses, and memoranda of things lent. Dorothy Ward's entries are daily and she uses the memoranda pages at the back of the 1890 volume to note expenditures and Bible passages as well as to make additional comments for some dates.
CONTENT: The two diary volumes of the unmarried daughter of Humphrey Ward and the novelist Mary Ward show the concerns of a well-educated young lady. The major theme in the 1890 diary is Dorothy's interest in music and her desire to perfect her piano-playing. In a number of entries she chastises herself over her inability to play well and show her preoccupation with others' fine performances, for she critiques public concerts as well as the accomplishments of her friends. One of her most important friendships is formed via music; female companionship constitutes a significant role in both her diary volumes. It is very important to Dorothy when she is asked by another young lady to call her by her first name. Yet another noteworthy event for Dorothy is her first dinner party, as this symbolizes growing up and her acceptance into the social circle of the intelligentsia which includes Leslie Stephen and Edmund Gosse. Dorothy acts as a secretary for her parents, especially

her mother, and she frequently attends lectures, studies German, and reads important novels such as <u>Great Expectations</u> and <u>Henry Esmond</u>.

Dorothy's frustration over her inability to behave properly and her anxiety over marriage is replaced in the 1898 volume by her habitual service to others. Much of the material in this diary has to do with Dorothy's work at the Passmore Edwards Settlement, a school for children. Dorothy organizes many of the school outings, keeps track of expenditures incurred in managing the settlement, and instructs the students. She also nurses sick relatives, especially her mother. The service women provide to each other during illnesses or crises indicates the primary role of female companionship in the lives of Victorian women. Dorothy is especially anxious, for example, about the stress undergone by a friend whose husband is fighting in Khartoum. The publication of her mother's novels is important to Dorothy, since she notes the kind of reception they receive; and she mentions, too, the family's acquisition of two Burne-Jones paintings which she considers beautiful. Both volumes contain accounts of trips she took to Ireland, Paris, and Italy; the second volume in particular shows her full life. She continued her diary keeping until 1955.

STYLISTIC FEATURES: The generally brief entries are written in pencil, though remarks about journeys are inscribed in ink. Occasionally in the 1890 volume she notes that nothing particular has occurred, but in the 1898 volume her sentence fragments, run-on words, and hurried penmanship betoken her hectic life. Sometimes she uses French phrases and designates expletives she does not want to record by dashes for the letters they contain. She frequently omits the personal pronoun, and in the 1898 volume writes that she has been "self-y" if she has not served others.

R1.
ROWNTREE, ELIZABETH (b. 1763, d. ?), Friends' Society Library, London, Box T.
DATE AND LOCATION: May, 1808-October, 1835, with many gaps. Scarborough, North Yorkshire; London.
FORMAT: 16 volumes. All of these volumes, which have been bound together in a blue volume labeled "memorandums," are diaries with printed formats. Of the three varieties in this collection, two are specially designed for Quakers in accordance with the Quaker calendar. One of the diaries printed for the Quakers is the 1808 <u>Memorandum</u> volume, which is characterized by the numerical designation of months and days of the week and the omission of the names of the months and days. In this volume there are spaces for days first through fourth on the verso page and for days fifth through seventh, plus an additional space, on the recto page. The month and the number of days in that month are printed at the top of the left-hand page, while the week is listed at the top

of the right-hand page. The dates and day of the week are designated on each page's left margin; and events important to Quakers are printed next to the appropriate dates.

Fourteen of the volumes are <u>Annual</u> <u>Monitors</u>, which feature mottos extracted from devotional works and which are also characterized by numerical designations for months and days. The verso page of the <u>Annual</u> <u>Monitor</u> is divided into quarters with a motto inscribed at the top, and the three additional spaces on the page are designed for the entries of the first through third days. The recto page contains spaces for the remaining days of the week. The numerical designation of the month is printed at the top of the left-hand page, while at the top of the right-hand page the number of the week is listed. The days of the week run along the left-hand edge of each page.

The 1811 volume is the third variety of diary with a printed format in this collection. Here the verso page contains spaces for all the week's entries while the recto page is for accounts. At the top of the left-hand page are printed the month, the number of days in the month, the position of that month within the year, and finally the year. The accounts page is divided into three vertical columns labeled "received," "amount of cash," and "paid or lent;" each of the columns is subdivided into partitions for pounds, shillings, and pence. The diarist uses the accounts page to write about events rather than to keep track of monetary expenditures.

Throughout the sixteen volumes Elizabeth Rowntree writes entries whenever she wishes to note important occurrences; consequently, her account is not daily. Frequently, a single entry will extend over the spaces allotted for several entries, so that there is not necessarily a correlation between the printed dates and the dates of the diarist's entries. This tendency is expecially marked in the earlier volumes.

CONTENT: The record, which was written by a Quaker missionary whose husband kept a shop, details her activities with the Church as well as the misfortunes of her family. Many of her entries record her travels to attend Quaker meetings in London or to visit Quaker families. Her comments about her journeys are reminiscent of travelogues, since she notes where she went, who she met, and what she ate, but she also evaluates her spiritual state during her journeys. One of her primary concerns when spreading the Quaker faith is the waywardness of children. Many were not adhering to the practices of their religion, but those who did were a source of joy and hope. Much of the time she spends visiting families is employed in admonishing parents to counsel their children.

She is also wary of increasing worldliness, especially in her son William, a mill owner. Her sense of the conflict between her duty to God and to her family is evident throughout the volumes, and she continually seeks God's help in overcoming this sensation. One of the clearest expressions of her feelings occurs when her daughter's illness prevents her from attending a monthly meeting. Her daughter Jane eventually dies in 1821 from consumption, as do two more of her daughters. Jane's dying requests and the responses they elicit are recorded by her mother, who considers Jane's acceptance of God's will as exemplary. The death of Jane is the first in a series of losses recorded in the diary volumes. Shortly after Jane's death the diarist's mother dies, and in 1824 Elizabeth Rowntree writes the account of her daughter Mary's death from tuberculosis. However, it is 1827 which is especially punctuated with death, for in this year both her husband and daughter Hannah die, the latter from convulsions. The death of her husband of forty-two years especially affects Elizabeth Rowntree and she beseeches God to aid her through her tribulations. The notation of the anniversary of his burial and her wedding, which coincide, become standard features in her record and a time for reflection, as is the end of each year.

As she grows older the diarist becomes increasingly concerned about being prepared for death and increasingly preoccupied with loss. She feels despondent when friends leave to become Quaker missionaries and when her daughter Elizabeth marries, since both events entail trying separations for the diarist, even though she realizes that both represent God's will. In 1833 her daughter Elizabeth dies from consumption, and by this point in her life the diarist feels very grateful whenever she sees a friend.

STYLISTIC FEATURES: The fairly long entries record important events. Many words are misspelled and sentences are run together and incorrectly punctuated. Sometimes she writes words or parts of words above others because she runs out of space or remembers to add words later. She uses dialogue when recording deathbed conversations, and she initials particularly significant entries such as the accounts of family deaths.

R2.
ANONYMOUS OF EDINBURGH (b. ?, d. ?), National Library of Scotland MS. 1658.
DATE AND LOCATION: January-March, 1813. Edinburgh.
FORMAT: The gray pocketbook volume has a red spine. There are daily entries with some summary entries. Since the diary ends after the death of the writer's mother, there are blank pages at the end of the volume.
CONTENT: This diary of a very religious and apparently middle-class girl is kept at the time of her communion and during the final illness of her mother. It was intended by its writer to be an instrument of character reformation. The diarist frequently writes of her inability to employ her time wisely or to pay strict attention in church; both her prayers to God and her rendition of her failings are an attempt to change such practices. She views women in the Bible, as well as many women she meets, as Christian exemplars. One of her most poignant

accounts is about the beauty of an invalid's death. The diarist considers the death beautiful both because the invalid's life of patient suffering followed Christian precepts and because her death frees her from travail and allows her to join Jesus. The writer fervently asks God to impress the deathbed scene of the invalid on her mind, so that she can never forget how beautiful she looked in death, nor fail to recall such a perfect example of the suffering of women.

The writer considers diary reading an activity which can encourage Christian behavior, for it reveals the motives and actions of exalted human beings. Her mother feels writing properly is a duty to God and chides her daughter when the diarist uses too many adjectives. The diarist's entries laud God's daily goodness and indicate her own desire to carry the Christian message through district visiting.

Much of the last part of the diary records the deathbed conversations of the writer's mother, who is apparently stricken with tuberculosis. Her deathbed becomes a consecrated spot where her children and her female friends gather. One of the mother's last requests is that after she dies she be left in her room as long as possible, and that when she is buried the graveyard will be watched. Presumably the mother was worried about premature burial and grave robbers. The diary account ends with the mother's death.

STYLISTIC FEATURES: The long, complex sentences are

punctuated with many commas. The entries are intended to celebrate the Lord and make the writer a better disciple. When recording her mother's deathbed conversations, the diarist quotes her mother.

R3.
WILMORE, LOUISA E. (b. ?, d. 1839), Wigan Record Office M962 EHC 170.
DATE AND LOCATION: 1814-37. Worcester and Hay, Hereford and Worcester.
FORMAT: The cloth-covered volume has a marbled surface and contains paper watermarked 1819. The entries between 1814 and 1822 are retrospective overviews of those years. Between 1823 and 1836 the entries are daily, while the entries for 1836 and 1837 are yearly. The daily entries are not always consecutive.
CONTENT: The diary, which was kept by the woman who married her childhood sweetheart, Reverend Edward W. Foley, in 1837, records her numerous losses and her spiritual struggles. The overview entries principally note marriages and deaths of relatives, though she also seems obsessed with violent deaths which are reported to her, for she describes these in some detail. She tells of one woman who committed suicide by throwing herself into a vat of boiling water, and of another woman who died after jumping from a carriage pulled by runaway horses. Her brother John's death in 1825 is followed by her father's in 1827. The latter's demise precipitates

the break-up of the family, an event which intensifies the acute sense of loss expressed by the diarist. In 1829 she forms a deeply emotional and spiritual friendship with Fanny, an invalid who dies in 1832. This is the year after the death of Molly, the family servant of thirty years.

Her sister Emily's death in 1833 signals a turning point in the diary, since after this the journal becomes more profusely religious, as the diarist becomes more conscious of her own illnesses and mortality. She frequently nurses other women, attends missionary meetings, and teaches Sunday School. Visiting the haunts of her childhood reminds her of the painful losses she has experienced and of the transcience of life. She turns increasingly to God, Whom she beseeches to help her through life's trials, including those occasioned by marriage proposals. Her oblique references to proposals indicate that the diarist was concerned about unconsciously encouraging attentions from men and that she conceived of the separation marriage precipitated as similar to the parting occasioned by death. She writes of the imprisonment enforced by the doctor because of her ill health. Her final entries in particular show her spiritual self-doubt.

STYLISTIC FEATURES: The heightened religious language is characterized by appeals addressed to God and by self-admonishments. When her entries are more regular they also become more cryptic, abbreviated, and fragmented.

Her language is especially oblique when she mentions marriage proposals.

R4.
WILLIAMS, HANNAH (b. ?, d. ?), National Library of Wales, Ty Coch 42 Add. MSS. 856A.
DATE AND LOCATION: October, 1816-March, 1817. Llanryng, Wales.
FORMAT: The pasteboard volume is covered with marbled paper and possesses a leather spine. The inside pages, which are lined horizontally with blue and vertically with red, indicate that this is an account book. The inside front cover is inscribed with the diarist's name and the date.
CONTENT: The diary kept by the wife, apparently of a clergyman, contains entries which enumerate daily activities and expenses. Many of the entries cite gifts of food received or given, household provisions prepared, and gifts to the poor distributed. The diarist notes the weather conditions as well as birthdays and significant outings. One of her few detailed entries describes the death of a mare who drove a stake into her own eye and a fall resulting in injury for the diarist.
STYLISTIC FEATURES: The terse entries signify that this diary is primarily an extension of an account book.

R5.
CROOME, MARGARET ANNE (b. ?, d. ?), Gloucestershire

Record Office D1183.

DATE AND LOCATION: 1823-24, with gaps; 1829. Bourton-on-the-Water and Cirencester, Gloucestershire.

FORMAT: The leather-covered volume is inscribed on the inside front cover with the diarist's name and the date. The entries for 1823 and 1824 are kept in the same volume as those for 1829. However, the 1829 entries begin from the back of the volume, whose inside rear cover is inscribed with the diarist's name and the date "1829." The entries are usually not dated but only signified by the day of the week.

CONTENT: The entries for 1823 and 1824 depict the daily life of the young daughter of the Reverend John Croome. Margaret writes about family acquisitions such as picture frames or bookcases, but she also describes her own pursuits, which include attending teas and dances, and getting new clothes. She frequently uses her journal to keep track of what she wears or to list visitors, though she also writes about illnesses, births, deaths, and marriages. She contracts the chicken pox and scarlatina, acts as a bridesmaid at her aunt's wedding, remarks on the birth of her younger sister, and bemoans the deaths of a neighbor's two children within a week. Interestingly, many of her comments in 1823 and 1824 refer to diaries. When she does not write in her journal, she gives lack of time as the excuse, though she chides herself for failing to record events since then she forgets them. She also mentions copying out Elizabeth Woodeville's diary. Her entries for 1824 end when she goes to boarding school.

Her 1829 entries also emphasize the importance of diaries, for here she notes reading a diary aloud to her younger sister, and expounds upon the reasons for maintaining one. She considers a diary an aid to moral reformation and concludes too that since diary keeping forces the writer to review her daily activities, the record exposes her follies. One of her more humorous entries recounts her farcical participation in theatricals as a Catholic priest. Toward the end of the 1829 entries she systematically chronicles her expenditures and her father's health.

STYLISTIC FEATURES: The entries are sporadically written in long sentences; sometimes the diarist omits the personal pronoun. Her 1829 entries show the influence of a boarding school education, since she uses French and Italian words.

R6.
PRINCE, MISS ELIZABETH (b. 1805, d. ?), Wigan Record Office D/DZ EHC 15 M783.
DATE AND LOCATION: May, 1830-April, 1831, with a break between December and March. Edge Hill, East Liverpool, Merseyside.
FORMAT: The small, bound, half-calf volume contains unruled pages. When she begins her first entry, the diarist lists dates and sometimes includes the day, month, and

year; at other times she lists only the day. The diary is interspersed with religious verse and recapitulations of sermons.

CONTENT: This diary of a twenty-five-year-old Church of England Sunday School teacher, whose dead father was a clergyman in a well-to-do Liverpool suburb, is purportedly begun as an aid to spiritual progress; and virtually every passage in the diary attests to her struggle between self and selflessness, between duty and desire. This struggle is most clearly borne out by the numerous instances in which she records her love for the Reverend Swainson, whom she fears will marry another, and the necessity of fighting against her idolization of him. She feels instead she should devote herself to God, although she obviously identifies Swainson with the latter and with her dead brother, who was to have been a clergyman.

The diary also records her rejection of an unworthy suitor, and indicates her tendency to see righteous individuals, whether in the Bible or on her round of philanthropic visits to the dying, as exemplars of piety. She distributes religious tracts, condemns the slave trade because it demoralizes the slave and makes the master a demon, and orders her household tasks so that her professed spiritual duties, including her diary writing, can take priority. She feels conflict between her duty to her only living parent and her spiritual progress when her mother asks her to curtail her diary

writing. After the death of her beloved elder sister, which causes a long break in her diary, she acts as her nephew's surrogate mother. She mentions the coming of the railroad first with awe and then with ambivalence, a sequence of emotions which is common in her diary.
STYLISTIC FEATURES: The diary is written in long, involved sentences or clauses and characteristically punctuated with semi-colons. When the subject is the diarist, the subject of the sentence is often omitted. The diary is directly addressed to God, and after her sister's death, to the latter's spirit. The entries for Sunday are longer than for other days of the week.

R7.
BUCHANAN, ELIZABETH (b. ?, d. ?), National Library of Scotland MS. 9981.
DATE AND LOCATION: 1837-41, with entries for only half of March, 1837, and with a gap between December, 1841, and June, 1843. Cambersmore, Scotland.
FORMAT: This small pasteboard volume has a red spine and a brown mottled cover. The white pages are lined and have spaces running down the left-hand side for entering the date and down the right-hand side for keeping accounts. The volume is inscribed with the diarist's name and the location. Daily entries are followed by summary entries for each month. There are also yearly summaries.
CONTENT: This is principally a diary of the weather,

which is kept by the youngest daughter of John Buchanan, rector of Amprior in Scotland. Although the diarist's stated purpose is to record the variations in weather, she also notes visits, political events, births, marriages, and deaths. Her monthly summaries contain information about the lives of her acquaintances. Eulogies are a common feature of her monthly summaries.

Her diary ends abruptly with a synopsis which indicates that she was unable to continue her record because of deaths in her family. Here she also lists the deaths of friends and the dates of other important events, as well as some weather reports which may indicate an attempt to continue her diary.

STYLISTIC FEATURES: The terse entries generally reveal little about the writer.

R8.

POWELL, LAVINIA (b. 1831, d. 1856), National Library of Wales, G. E. Evans Bequest MS. 13, 345. See also Powell, Ophelia Catherine, and Powell, Delia.

DATE AND LOCATION: February, 1840-April, 1849; December, 1854-May, 1856. Colyton, near Exeter, Devon.

FORMAT: The pressboard pocket volume, which has a marbled brown cover and a spine inscribed with the diarist's initials and the dates of her journal, apparently contains two separate diaries which have been bound together. The pages of the first diary have blue lines drawn across them and a line running down the left-hand side.

The diarist uses the left-hand margin to note the month and the date of her entries which are very occasional, though they become more frequent after 1843. In the second diary the blue lines only run horizontally, and here the writer only makes entries on holidays or anniversaries.

CONTENT: Written by the daughter of the Royal Navy Commander George Eyre Powell, the first diary describes noteworthy events in her life and that of her family. These include her father's military activities, the arrival and departure of daily governesses, the illnesses and death of her grandmother, the acquisition of family possessions such as a grand piano, and the baptism of her sisters and herself. After her acceptance into the church, the diarist becomes a Sunday School teacher. She visits the ailing and distributes charity. She uses her diary to note the agitations of the village poor. There is some mention of political events, for Lavinia comments on the French revolution of 1848 and the Chartists' assemblage in London. The coming of the railroad is a significant local occurrence, as are outbreaks of fire. Her second diary is a record of her spiritual state. She consistently finds herself wanting in her desire to serve God, and she repeatedly compares the inferiority of her conduct to the exemplary behavior of Jesus.

STYLISTIC FEATURES: Her entries in the first diary are short and show little reaction to events. An exception is the lengthy and detailed entry which describes her grandmother's death. The long entries in the second diary indicate her religiosity and self-examination.

R9.
BLATHWAYT, FRANCES ELIZABETH (b. 1830, d. ?), Gloucestershire Record Office, Dyrham Park MSS D1799, F249-259. See also Blathwayt, Mrs. W. T., and Blathwayt, Mrs. W. E.
DATE AND LOCATION: 1849-53, 1858, 1860, 1861-62, 1864-68, with brief gaps. Weybridge, Surrey; Langridge, Somerset; Pau, France.
FORMAT: 11 volumes. Some volumes are leather covered; others have marbled paper covers. The pages are lined with faint blue ink, and the volumes are inscribed with the diarist's name and the date. The 1864 volume is a <u>Harwood's Diary</u>, and three volumes are Letts's diaries. The contents of the Letts's diaries include calendars of public holidays, eclipses, English fairs, and university terms; tables for interest reckoning, foreign money, and the weather; listings of London and country bankers, birthdays of the royal family, houses of Peers and Commons, life assurance companies, and army and navy agents. At the front of the volume there are advertisements for other Letts's publications. In one Letts's volume there are spaces for three or four daily entries per page, but in another volume one half-page is allotted per day with a whole page allowed for Saturday. Her volumes contain a number of short gaps which were caused

by illness, childbirth, or a professed lack of interesting events.

In the self-constructed volumes the diarist notes the place of composition at the top of the page, and her volumes sometimes contain records of expenditures, books loaned or read, and letters written, as well as notations of births, deaths, and marriages of public figures, family members, and parishioners. Her entries begin with the day and the date and sometimes the month.

CONTENT: The diary kept by Frances Elizabeth Blathwayt, the wife of the rector of Langridge, begins with her account of her marriage at nineteen. She describes in detail her wedding, which is characterized by the flowers strewn everywhere, and remarks that marriages are so melancholy that she is grateful for their rare occurrence. The volumes chronicle the family and social events of her class, such as badger and fox hunting, day-school superintendence, and the tenants' dinner, and note too the marriages, births, and illnesses of various relatives. Parts of her diary describe her honeymoon sojourn in France, and her travels in England.

An especially interesting feature of this diary is its account of childbirth, as Frances Elizabeth Blathwayt describes the births of her three sons and the illnesses associated with each. She is quite overjoyed when the births go well. The volumes detail the activities of her sons, such as the plans for their education and their parties. Accounts of the latter are intriguing because of their class and racial bias. On her second son's first birthday he presides at the head of a table of seventy-seven school children, after being drawn in a carriage covered with evergreens and roses; and her son Georgie entertains school children after Christmas by dressing like a Negro and singing several Negro melodies.

Illnesses of the children, servants, relatives, and parishioners show the extent to which disease regulated the diarist's activities, for a severe bout of influenza in the household forced Mrs. Blathwayt to perform tasks usually done by servants. Few political events are mentioned, though she does refer to a local victory of the Conservatives in 1865. When she describes her reactions to attending the Great Exhibition in 1851, she says how impressed she is by the architecture of the building. Later in her journal she mourns the death of Prince Albert. She notes when she wrote in her diary while traveling, and remarks on hearing the diary of a foreign tour read aloud while she and her friends drew.
STYLISTIC FEATURES: Her detailed entries are generally written in long, complex sentences, though often she uses fragments to comment about the weather and omits the first-person personal pronoun. She sometimes writes in pencil which is then marked over in ink.

R10.

POWELL, OPHELIA CATHERINE (b. 1823, d. 1866), National Library of Wales, G. E. Evans Bequest, MSS No. 13-15.

See also Powell, Delia, and Powell, Lavinia.

DATE AND LOCATION: July, 1849-July, 1864. Colyton, near Exeter, Devon; Exeter; London; Carmarthen, Dyfed, Wales.

FORMAT: Three volumes. The first of these volumes is large and made of blue mottled pasteboard with a brown spine. The spine is embossed in gold with the diarist's initials and the dates of her work. The pages are lined and the first few are blank. The second volume has been rebound in red and the diarist's name is inscribed in gold on the spine. The pages are light blue and faintly lined, and the writer has inscribed her name, location, and the date inside the volume. The third volume is pocketbook size and is labeled with the diarist's initials and the years covered by the volume.

The entries are daily in the first volume, which covers 1849 to 1852, and here the diarist enters the month initially and then only the dates of the month. Her entries are irregular in the second volume where she notes the day of the week and the date beside her entries. This volume runs from 1852 to 1864 and is a chronological continuation of the first volume. The third volume, which merely lists the dates when books and handiwork were completed, is kept between 1850 and 1855.

CONTENT: Two of the diary volumes, which were kept by the daughter of George Eyre Powell, a commander in the Royal Navy, and the wife of Reverend Professor David Lewis Evans, detail her personal life. The third volume merely notes when she finished pieces of handiwork and what she read, which includes _Guy Mannering_, _Uncle Tom's Cabin_, Boswell's _Life of Johnson_, Blair's _Sermons_, the Sunday School magazine, and stories written for young women.

Ophelia begins her diary because she wants to record the main events of each week and because she is leaving home for the first time. The occasion of her short journey to Exeter sets the mood of the first volume and presages much of its material, for the major theme of this volume is Ophelia's fear of change. During the span covered by this volume Ophelia travels to Exeter several times and to London, and in each place she visits the major sights. The Great Exhibition especially excites her admiration, though she comments more extensively about her attendance at the church services of different religious groups, since these afford a contrast to her own Unitarianism. While she is at home Ophelia's time is employed in completing domestic chores, nursing sick relatives, teaching Sunday School, distributing tracts, and attending the lectures offered by the local Mutual Improvement Society. However, the major event of the volume is the marriage proposal of the Reverend Evans, since this creates contradictory sensations which Ophelia expresses in her diary. Although Ophelia feels that being a Unitarian minister's wife is a sacred and important duty, she nevertheless regrets leaving home and breaking the family bond. Frequently when she reviews her past or writes anniversary entries, Ophelia considers the dilemma represented by the change marriage implies and attempts to overcome her fears by asserting the positive aspects of her union with the Reverend Evans.

The second volume begins with a long description by the diarist of her village residence and immediate family as well as of herself, since she wishes the future reader to be acquainted with her situation. In the first part of this volume Ophelia continues to elucidate her daily life and concerns, and to be preoccupied with the changes which will be wrought by marriage. The actual fitting of the wedding ring causes Ophelia to feel great apprehension and many misgivings, but the sensations of change which this act symbolizes are overshadowed by the real loss occasioned by her father's death in 1855. She pictures the actual death of her father, including his last words and final kiss; and during her wedding ceremony in 1856, she cries because she cannot help but remember her beloved father. Ophelia's sense of her altered position after her marriage is represented by her references to her partner as "dear husband" instead of Mr. Evans, and by her cognizance of now being a visitor in the parental home.

The remainder of the diary is punctuated by change. Between 1856 and 1863 Ophelia's mother and two of her sisters die, and Ophelia gives birth to four children. Although none of these deaths are as fully detailed as that of her father, Ophelia regards her mother's death as especially melancholy since it necessitates the break-up of the family home. A very interesting feature of Ophelia's account is her commentary about childbirth and its aftereffects. She is relieved and thankful to hear the sound of the doctor's carriage wheels at the time of her first child's birth in 1857; and when her fourth child is born in 1863 she notes her protracted recovery from the birth. Ophelia's diary ends when she moves to Carmarthen, where her husband must accept a professorship to support the growing family. The final entry describes their new home as damp and inconvenient. STYLISTIC FEATURES: Generally the entries are short, although when the diarist has many or contradictory reactions to events the entries are quite long. Only occasionally does she remark that she has nothing to record, although domestic duties sometimes prevent her from finding time to write. The second volume features a number of summary entries, since family deaths and childbirth keep the diarist from maintaining her record. She dates and signs important entries; and often her entries exhibit clear penmanship, some lack of punctuation, and run-on sentences.

R11.

POWELL, DELIA (b. 1832, d. 1923), Library of Wales, G. E. Evans Bequest MSS. 65-69. See also Powell, Lavinia, and Powell, Ophelia Catherine.

DATE AND LOCATION: November, 1856-June, 1894, with many gaps between October, 1862-December, 1864, January to

November, 1882, and December, 1883-May, 1894. Colyton, near Exeter, Devon.

FORMAT: Five volumes. The first volume, which covers 1856 to 1859, is a pasteboard maroon book with embossed covers and blue pages. Similar to volume one, the second volume runs from 1859-77. The third volume has pasteboard covers with green marbling and pages ruled in light blue ink; it runs from 1877 to 1894. The remaining two volumes contain rules composed by Delia for her conduct; the first of these begins in 1856, simultaneously with volume one of the principal diary, and continues until 1859 when the second volume of conduct rules commences. In 1862 the latter volume becomes a diary where she records her daily activities, while she continues to reserve the rendition of her reactions for the major diary volumes. The first volume of rules has green pasteboard covers and pages ruled in blue ink. The second rules volume, which has pasteboard covers and stitch binding, appears to be composed of three notebooks bound together. The pages of the notebooks have ruled blue lines, but the diarist has drawn a vertical central line on each page so that there are two columns. The second rules volume ends in 1866.

Her first volume contains irregularly kept entries, while the second volume merely notes events of particular importance. In 1871 the diarist begins monthly summaries, and in 1872 the diary is transformed into a yearly summary. By 1876 she is again writing entries when noteworthy events occur. The entries in the third volume are irregularly kept until she reverts to monthly summaries in 1879. When she begins in early 1862 making daily entries in the second rules volume, she writes these regularly until her mother's death in August of 1862, at which point the entries become much more sporadic.

CONTENT: The diary volumes, which were maintained by the daughter of George Eyre Powell, a commander in the Royal Navy, were begun because the writer wanted to examine her conduct. Delia starts both her principal volume and her rules volume in November because this is the beginning of her personal year, the month of her birthday. The rules volume sets out the standards for her conduct, which principally involve abstinence in eating, service to others, and adherence to Christ's example. Delia proposes a self-review each Saturday as well as a daily reading of her regulations, and the first rules volume records how well she followed her self-prescriptions.

When Delia starts her main diary volume, she says that she wants to follow her dead father's example and asks for God's help, because whenever she reviews her past actions, she finds her behavior amiss. The reactions Delia records in her diary indicate her desire to be a good Christian and a useful human being, for she writes how significant for her are visiting the poor and nursing her sick relatives. She is upset by her family's failure to recognize her many services and their opposition to her giving music lessons. The conflicts with her family, which Delia mentions in the first main diary volume, presage later problems. Delia's repeated visits to loved ones' graves, her descriptions of deathbed scenes, and her notation of the anniversaries of personally significant deaths also occur throughout the diary volumes. Her sister Narcissa dies in 1858, and when her mother dies in 1862, she must leave the family home.

At the beginning of the second chief diary volume Delia says that she will only record major events, since her daily life varies so little. One such noteworthy occurrence is her relationship with Alexander McCombe, a Unitarian clergyman who wishes to marry her. However, when his attack of paralysis precludes any plans for marriage, Delia begins nursing him in her own cottage. She feels that God will vindicate her decision but realizes that her fellow human beings may damn her. Her relatives condemn Delia's behavior and attempt to remove her from her post as treasurer of the local chapel. Her diary records the ensuing conflict between Delia and her family. Eventually the matter is decided in court in Delia's favor. Delia nurses Alexander McCombe until his death in 1876 and later recalls his last moments each year by reading his sermons and visiting his grave. After his death Delia has two suitors who wish to marry her. Although initially she refuses both of them, she later accepts Samuel Rall's attentions until he dies while sitting next to her. As is usual in her entries about the deaths of loved ones, Delia describes the closing of his coffin as well as the burial. Delia declines yet another proposal. When her diary ends she is complaining of ill health as she has throughout her journal, commending herself to God from whom she asks forgiveness, and remembering the past.

The second rules volume, like the first one, records how strictly she adheres to her self-prescriptions. She notes when she feels God considers her worthy enough to suffer, since this signals joy in heaven, and when she is in harmony with the Sabbath. This volume also records her daily activities once she decides to keep it as a diary of her deeds.

STYLISTIC FEATURES: The entry length varies depending on whether the events are significant to the diarist. She writes run-on sentences. When personal or family conflicts occur the entries are often crossed out; and when highly significant events take place she often writes lengthy summary entries. The diarist refers to herself as "self," and when her relationships with her suitors become more intimate she calls them by their first names.

R12.
BLATHWAYT, MRS. W. T. (b. ?, d. 1925), Gloucestershire Record Office D1799/F260. See also Blathwayt, Frances Elizabeth, and Blathwayt, Mrs. W. E.

DATE AND LOCATION: 1879-81, with chronological omissions. Dyrham, Avon.

FORMAT: The black morocco-covered volume has stitch binding in poor condition and patterned inside covers. The pages are ruled in light blue lines. The diary often contains gaps of several months; some of the entries are incorrectly dated, and the volume is written by two amanuenses as well as by the diarist.

CONTENT: Written by the wife of the rector of Dyrham, the diary is largely about her ill health, especially her anxiety about her loss of sight and the operation to restore it. She also suffers from rheumatism and swollen glands, and her illnesses often keep her confined within the house. She mentions the weather and the visits she makes, many of which are to London doctors, and notes too the deaths and illness of friends and relatives.

Her diary is obviously very significant for her, since it is maintained by others when illness prevents the diarist from writing. Both her maid and her husband presumably act as her amanuensis, for the details of her declining eyesight are recorded by one hand and the description of her operation by another.

STYLISTIC FEATURES: This spottily-written diary is sometimes composed in pencil.

R13.
MOOR, F. D. (b. ?, d. ?), Wigan Record Office M924 EHC 139.

DATE AND LOCATION: April-June, 1890. London to Wiesbaden, Germany.

FORMAT: The black, stiff, cloth-covered volume contains heavy, unlined paper. A few pages have been removed and some pages at the end are blank. The diarist's inscription lists the date and briefly suggests the diary's contents. The pages are numbered and the entries sometimes cover several days. The entries are demarcated by the dates they cover and are daily.

CONTENT: The travel diary of the wife of the Reverend Frewen Moor, Vicar of Ampfield, Sussex, was maintained during a journey to Wiesbaden to consult an oculist about the Reverend's poor eyesight. Many of the entries describe Mrs. Moor's anxiety about her husband's condition, as well as the illnesses experienced by herself and her daughter Selina, who accompanied her parents on the trip. Selina suffers from neuralgia occasioned by the cold, while her mother frequently has palpitations of the heart, perhaps caused by worry over her husband's eye operation. The operation turns out to be a success. The cost of the operation, two weeks of room and board for the patient, and a tip, is only twenty pounds. Mrs. Moor complains of being obliged each day to read the Bible to her husband until her voice fails her and of his insistence that he keep the purse, even though his condition makes this impractical. Her husband is obviously inconsiderate and parsimonious, for he refuses to hire a carriage, either for sightseeing expeditions in Heidelberg and Schwalbach, or for his wife's health. The long walks he insists upon tire her greatly.

The diary contains numerous xenophobic comments. She writes of the monotony of Holland, the uncouthness of the German language, and the lack of manners exhibited by the Germans, who continually sip hot chicken broth, suck their bones like dogs, and feed young children oranges. She also condemns smokers, especially if they are women, and notes that the old men all seem to have young wives. One of her last entries alludes to the death of her son three years earlier. She closes her diary by expressing her thanks for their safe return home.

STYLISTIC FEATURES: The generally long entries recount the diarist's personal experiences and emotional states. Her sentences are long and filled with descriptive adjectives and examples.

R14.

BLATHWAYT, MRS. W. E. (b. ?, d. ?), Gloucestershire Record Office D1799/F282. See also Blathwayt, Frances Elizabeth, and Blathwayt, Mrs. W. T.

DATE AND LOCATION: 1893. Probably in Gloucestershire or Avon.

FORMAT: The volume has a black cloth cover embossed on the front with "Diary 1893." The inside front cover of this <u>Army and Navy Pocket Diary and Almanac</u> contains advertisements for black lead, investment companies, candles, mineral water, coca wine, artist's supplies, sports equipment, life assurance, carriages, coal, and diaries. At the back there are advertisements for lawn mowers, soups, stamps, bibles, and puddings. The printed contents comprise listings of notable political and military dates, ranks in the Army and Navy, London cab fares, and London daily and weekly newspapers. Interestingly, there is also advice about how properly to address officials and the gentry.

The volume exhibits a week at an opening, since the verso page is divided into Monday through Wednesday and the recto page shows Thursday through Sunday. Religious dates are noted; there is a cash accounts section for the year by month; and there are memoranda pages.
CONTENT: The entries kept by the wife of W. E. Blathwayt, later the rector of Dyrham and the son of Frances Elizabeth Blathwayt (q.v.), mainly describe the weather and the progress of the foliage and the garden. She marks when the currants ripen or when the hawthorns bloom. There are a few personal entries which note visits and marriages, such as the nuptials of family members and the Duke of York. The memoranda pages list recipes, especially for soups and venison.
STYLISTIC FEATURES: The entries are very short and sketchy.

R15.

DUNDAS, MARY W. (b. ?, d. ?), National Library of Scotland

MS. 14199.

DATE AND LOCATION: July, 1894. Albury, probably Surrey; Switzerland.

FORMAT: The black, leather-bound volume contains blue-lined white pages and is inscribed with the date and location. Some entries are summary notations; others are daily.

CONTENT: The daughter of the rector of Albury maintained this diary during her three-week journey to Switzerland. It is a well-written and entertaining account, since the writer's wry observations assess the essence of the situations she encounters from her own point-of-view. She quickly establishes herself as a perceptive and opinionated observer. For example, when she sees the poor in mourning on board ship, she expatiates upon the uselessness of such a custom, since it requires the living to sacrifice basic necessities.

The diarist describes her activities during her sojourn. These include mountain climbing, participating in intense discussions based on reading Browning, and writing diaries. She reports that her group spent a whole morning at the hotel composing letters and diaries and that young Betsy was particularly encouraged by her elders to keep her journal. Keeping a diary enabled Mary Dundas to assess changes in herself, since she notes that her ideas have altered during her trip; for example, she claims that she now prefers to view scenery without hearing the trite comments usually made about it.

STYLISTIC FEATURES: Some entries are largely reportage, but many show the diarist's narrative skill and humor. She uses slang expressions, such as "dead" for "tired."

INDEX OF DIARISTS

Anonymous (of Edinburgh): R2 (p. 93)

Anonymous (of Buckinghamshire): PC13 (p. 65)

Anonymous (of Hull): PC6 (p. 51)

Arrowsmith, Lady Louisa: A4 (p. 10)

Ashton, Marianne: A6 (p. 14)

Blathwayt, Frances Elizabeth: R9 (p. 104)

Blathwayt, Mrs. W. E.: R14 (p. 117)

Blathwayt, Mrs. W. T.: R12 (p. 114)

Brougham, Lady Marianne: A1 (p. 1)

Buchanan, Elizabeth: R7 (p. 101)

Capel, Lady Adela: A9 (p. 19)

Coates, Eliza: PC10 (p. 59)

Cowper, Lady Adine: A10 (p. 21)

Croome, Margaret Anne: R5 (p. 97)

Davis, Miss: G2 (p. 31)

Denman, Frances: A7 (p. 15)

De Rutzen, Baroness: A5 (p. 13)

Dickenson, Eliza: PC8 (p. 55)

Dundas, Mary W.: R15 (p. 118)

Estcourt, Marianne Harriet Bucknall: G4 (p. 34)

Fuller, Mrs. Juliana: G6 (p. 38)

Galton, Emma: I1 (p. 79)

Galton, Louisa: I2 (p. 81)

Grimston, Hon. Charlotte: A3 (p. 8)

Haslam, Sarah: PC1 (p. 41)

Holtzapfel, Charlotte: PC3 (p. 44)

Humphreys, Elizabeth: PC11 (p. 60)

Johnston, Jane: PC4 (p. 46)

Lapidge, Marianne: PC7 (p. 53)

Larmuth, Helena: PC19 (p. 76)

Lascelles, Hon. Frederica: A12 (p. 26)

Legatt, Frederica Constance: PC14 (p. 66)

Llwyngwain, Harriette Bowen: G7 (p. 39)

Lytton, Lady Edith: A13 (p. 28)

Mence, Sarah: PC9 (p. 58)

Miers, Mrs. S. M.: PC12 (p. 61)

Milford, Lady: A8 (p. 18)

Moor, F. D.: R13 (p. 115)

Polhill, Frances M.: G3 (p. 32)

Powell, Delia: R11 (p. 110)

Powell, Lavinia: R8 (p. 102)

Powell, Ophelia Catherine: R10 (p. 106)

Prince, Miss Elizabeth: R6 (p. 99)

Ramsden, Diana: PC20 (p. 77)

Reynolds, Lady R.: A11 (p. 24)

Rowntree, Elizabeth: R1 (p. 89)

Russell, Miss Helen: G5 (p. 36)

Simpson, L. M.: PC15 (p. 69)

Stevens, Eliza Hope (governess of): PC5 (p. 50)

Stewart, Mrs.: G1 (p. 29)

Stuart, T.: PC2 (p. 43)

Verey, Miss I. E.: PC17 (p. 73)

Verulam, Lady Charlotte: A2 (p. 6)

Ward, Dorothy Mary: I4 (p. 86)

Ward, Mary Augusta: I3 (p. 83)

Williams, Eleanor: PC18 (p. 75)

Williams, Hannah: R4 (p. 97)

Williams, Sarah: PC16 (p. 72)

Wilmore, Louisa E.: R3 (p. 95)

SUBJECT INDEX TO BIBLIOGRAPHY

Aborigines: PC20

Accounts:

   --ledgers in diaries: A1, A10, A12, G2, G7, PC4, PC10, PC13, PC16, R1, R4, R7, R14

   --noted by diarist: A1, A4, A6, A10, G2, G3, G7, PC4, PC6, PC8, PC13, PC16, I4, R4, R5, R9

Advertisements: A12, G7, PC7, PC18, I3, R9, R14

Amanuensis: R12

Architecture: A10, A11, PC1

Arley (village of): PC17

Army Agents (listed): A9, G7, PC4, PC13, I3, R9, R14

Arnold, Matthew (writer): I3

Arrowsmith, Edward (attorney): A4

Asceticism: A10

Audience (for diary): PC5, PC17, PC20, R10

Australia: PC20

Authorship: PC19, I1, I3

Bankers (listed): A9, A10, G7, PC4, PC7, I3, R9, R14

Bath: G6, PC2

Baynes, Sir Robert Lambert (admiral): A7

Bazaars: G5, PC6

Bedfordshire: G3

Subject Index

Beer (cost of): G7, PC4

Bees: PC16

Berkshire: PC17

Bible Reading: A7, PC2, I4, R6, R13

Birmingham: PC12

Births: A2, A3, G2, PC4, PC12, PC14, I1, I2, R5, R7

Blair's *Sermons*: R10

Blenheim: PC1

Boarding School: A1, R5

Boating: PC17

Botany: A3

Boycott, William (businessman): PC3

Brazil: PC12

Brighton: PC6, PC14, PC15

British Museum: A11, PC10, PC12

Brontë, Charlotte (novelist): PC12

Brooker's Club: A8

Brougham, Lord Henry (statesman): A1, A7

Browning, Robert (poet): R15

Buckinghamshire: PC13

Bulwer-Lytton, Edward George (author): A13

Burne-Jones, Sir Edward (painter): I4

Business Management: G3, PC14, PC16

Byron, Lord (poet): A10, PC12

Cab Fares (listed): A1, A6, A9, G2, G3, PC4, PC7, PC13, I3, R14

Cambridge: A10

Canals: PC17

Cancer: PC2

Carlyle, Thomas (writer): PC12

Carrington, Lord: PC1

Catholic Question: A3

Catholicism: A10, I1, R5

Cato Street Conspiracy: A4

Cattle Shows: A11, PC12

Charity: A1, A4, A10, A12, G4, PC3, PC14, I3, R3, R4, R6, R8, R10, R11

Chartism: R8

Childbirth: A1, A2, PC3, PC8, PC12, R9, R10

Child Rearing: A2, A12, A13, G3, PC3, PC5, PC12, R1

China: A10

Cholera: G4, PC8

Church Attendance: A2, A4, A5, A10, A11, PC6, R1, R6, R8, R10, R11

Churching: A2

Class Distinctions: A3, A4, A10, A13, G5, PC14

Clergy:
    --wives of: R3, R4, R9, R10, R12, R13, R14
    --daughters of: R5, R6, R7, R15

Coal (cost of): PC4

Code (diary written in): G5

Coleridge, Samuel Taylor (poet): A10

Conservatives: R9

Country Houses: A11, G5

Courtship: A1, A7, PC10, R3, R6, R10, R11

Cowper, 6th Earl of: A10

SUBJECT INDEX

Crimean War: G4, G5

Crystal Palace: A11, PC12, I1

Cumbria: A1, G2

Currency Tables: A1, A6, PC7

Czar: G5

Dante Alighieri (Italian poet): A10

Day School: A2, A7, G4, PC9, PC14, R9

Death (fear or adulation of): A7, A10, G3, G4, PC8, PC14, PC15, I2, R1, R2, R3, R11

Deaths:
    --described fully: A4, A7, G4, PC8, PC14, PC15, I1, R1, R2, R3, R8, R10, R11
    --noted briefly: A4, A12, G3, G7, PC4, PC14, PC16, PC18, I1, I2, R3, R5, R9, R11, R12, R13

Denman, Thomas (Lord Chief Justice): A7

Denmark, Princess of: A5

Dental Problems: A2, PC11, PC12

De Quincey, Thomas (essayist): PC12

Derbyshire: A7, G4

Devon: A10, G6, R8, R10, R11

Dialogue (used in diaries): A3, A7, PC7, R1, R2

Diaries:
    --advertisements for: G7, PC7, PC18, I3, R14
    --printed format: A3, A6, A9, A10, A12, G2, G3, G7, PC2, PC4, PC7, PC13, I3, I4, R1, R9, R14
    --read by diarist: A10, G4, G5, PC8, PC12, R2, R5

Diary-Keeping Impulse: A1, A3, A5, G4, G5, PC5, PC8, PC9, PC12, R2, R5, R6, R10, R15

Dickens, Charles (novelist): PC12, PC14

Dickenson, Thomas (colonel): PC8

Diction (used in diaries):

    --novelistic: A7, PC12

    --poetic: PC1, I2

    --religious: R3

Dioramas: PC6

Diplomats: A13

Dog Fees: G3, G7, I3

Dogs: A8, A11, G4, PC15, PC20

Don Quixote: A7

Dover: A1

Durham: PC2

Eardley-Wilmot, John: PC1

Eclipse Calendars: R9

Education: A2, A7, A12, G3, G4, PC5, PC7, PC9, PC12, PC14, PC20, I4, R5, R9, R10

Eglinton, Earl of: A9

Engineering: PC8, PC12

Entertainments:

    --described by diarist: A1, A3, A7, G3, G6, PC3, PC7, PC12, PC14, PC20

    --printed in diaries: A1, G2, PC7, PC13

Equestrian Skills: PC19, PC20

Essex, Earl of: A9

Estcourt, James: G4

Etiquette: PC5, R14

Eulogies: A4, R7

SUBJECT INDEX 129

Evans, Prof. David Lewis: R10

Evelina: A7

Exemplars: PC8, R2, R6, R8, R11

Exhibitions (artistic): A4, A10, A11, A13, G3, PC3

Eyeglasses (cost of): G7

Factories: PC2

Fairs:

    --listed: R9

    --mentioned: A4, PC18

Family Relationships of Diarist:

    --with children: A1, A2, A10, A11, A12, A13, G3, PC3, PC4, PC5, PC12, I3, R1

    --with husband: A1, A4, A12, PC3, PC10, PC12, I2, I3, R1, R10

    --with other relatives: A3, A4, A7, G3, G5, I1, I2, I4, PC3, PC12, PC15, R3, R6, R11

    --with parents: A1, A3, A7, A10, G4, G5, PC3, PC12, PC14, PC19, I1, I2, I4, R1, R3, R6, R10, R11

    --with siblings: A1, A3, A7, A10, G4, G5, PC3, PC7, PC14, PC19, I1, I2, R3, R6, R10, R11

Fane, Julian Henry Charles: A10

Farming: A2, A4, PC13, PC18

Fashion: G1, R5

Female Friendships: A9, A10, G5, PC3, PC8, PC12, PC14, I1, I2, I4, R3

Financial Difficulties: PC15, I1

Fires: R8

Fisheries, Inspector of: A12

Foodstuffs: G7, PC4, PC16

Fox Hunting: R9

France: A1, A5, A6, A10, A11, A13, G4, I3, I4, R9

Frederick, George Augustus: A10

French Revolution of 1848: R8

Funerals: A4, R11

Galton, Francis (scientist): I1, I2

Galton, Samuel T. (banker): I1

Gambling: A1, PC4

Gardening: A9, A11, I3, R14

Gas Lighting: A4

George III: A2, A4, PC4

George IV: A1, A2, A3, A4, PC3

German Language: I4, R13

Germany: R13

Gladstone, W. E. (politician): A10, I2, I3

Gloucestershire: A1, A11, G4, PC1, PC6, PC8, PC10, PC15, R5, R9, R12, R14

God (addressed in diaries): A1, A2, A4, A10, G3, PC15, R1, R2, R3, R6, R11

Goethe, Wolfgang von (German poet): PC12

Gordon, Gen. Charles George: A12, I2

Gosse, Edmund (writer): I4

Governesses: PC5, R8

Grammar (improper use in diaries): A4, A9, PC3, PC18, I4, R1, R10, R11

Great Exhibition of 1851: PC14, I1, R9, R10

Great Expectations: I4

SUBJECT INDEX 131

Grimston, James Walter (3rd Viscount): A2, A3

Guy Mannering: R10

Hair Powder (duty on): G3

Hanoverian Succession: A3

Hawthorne, Nathaniel (American writer): PC12

Haydon, Benjamin Robert (painter): A4

Hebrew: A3

Henry Esmond: I4

Herefordshire: R3

Hertfordshire: A2, A3, A4, A10, I3, I4

Holidays (listed): A6, G3, G7, PC4, PC7, R14

Holland: A7, R13

Home Rule Bill: I3

Honeymoons: G6, PC3, PC12

Horse Racing: A1

Household Management: A2, A4, G7, PC2, PC4, PC8, PC11, PC13, PC19, PC20, I2, I4, R4, R6, R10

Humor: G1, R5, R15

Hunt, Henry (orator): A3, A4

Huxley, Thomas (biologist): I3

Idylls of the King: PC14

Illness:

    --of others described by diarist: A2, A4, A8, A12, G2, G4, PC3, PC8, PC12, I1, I2, I4, R1, R3, R5, R8, R9, R11, R12, R13

    --of diarist: A1, A2, A3, A8, G3, PC3, PC4, PC12, I1, I2, R3, R4, R5, R9, R11, R12, R13

Illuminations: A1, A3, PC3, PC14

Illustrations: A1, A3, G4, G6, PC1, PC6, PC7, PC13, PC14, PC17, PC20

India: PC8

Interest Tables: A9, G2, G3, PC7, PC10, PC13, PC18, R9

Ireland: A6, PC15, I3, I4, R9

Irish Reform Bill: A7

Isle of Man: PC19

Isle of Wight: A10, A11, G4, PC15

Italy: A1, G4, I4

Johnston, Henry George: PC4

Kean, Edmund (actor): A8

Khartoum: A12, I2, I4

Laborers: G5, PC2

Lace (cost of): PC4

Lancashire: A12, PC19

Lapidge, Edward (architect): PC7

Lawyers: A4, G3, PC4, PC11

Lectures (public): G5, PC3, PC14, I4, R10

Lessing, Gotthold Ephraim (German writer): A10

Life of Johnson: R10

Light Brigade, Charge of the: G4

Liverpool: R6

London: A1, A2, A3, A7, A8, A9, A10, A11, A12, G3, G4, PC1, PC3, PC4, PC6, PC10, PC11, PC12, PC14, PC15, I2, I3, I4, R1, R10, R13

Longfellow, Henry Wadsworth (American poet): A10

Loss, sense of: G4, PC8, PC15, I1, R1, R3, R10, R13

Louis XVIII (of France): PC3

Subject Index

Lunatics (cost of): G7

Lytham (village): G2

Lytton, Edward Robert (diplomat): A13

Macaulay, Thomas Babington (historian): PC12

McCombe, Alexander (minister): R11

Macready, William (actor): A8

Malvern Hills: PC17

Manchester: PC19

Mangnall, Richard (educator): PC9

Marriages (recorded): A4, A12, PC14, I1, I2, R3, R5, R7, R14

Married Law Defense Union: G7

Martineau, Harriet (author): A7

Matrimony (discussed by diarist): A3, G1, PC3, PC8, PC14, PC15, I4, R3, R10, R11

Medical Practices: A1, A2, G3, G4, PC2, PC3, PC8, PC12, R10, R13

Medievalism: A10

Middlesex: PC6, PC7, I1

Migration: A1, PC12, PC14, PC20

Military: A10, G4, PC1, PC8, R8, R10, R11

Milton, John (poet): A10

Missionary Work: A4, A12, R1, R3

Monuments (funereal): A3

Moral Conduct: A7, PC5, PC8, PC19, I4, R1, R2, R3, R5, R6, R8, R11

Mountain Climbing: R15

Mourning: A1, A4, G4, PC8, PC15, R3, R11, R15

Music: A7, A9, PC7, I4

Mutual Improvement Society: R10

Napoleon: A3, A11, PC2

Narratives: A3, A7, A10, G1, G4, PC14, R2, R15

National Gallery: A11, PC6

Nelson, Horatio (admiral): A1

Newspapers:

    --listed: G7, R14

    --mentioned by diarist: A12, G4, PC20

Nightingale, Florence (nurse): G4

Novels: PC12, PC14, PC15, PC20, I3, I4

Nursing (of sick): A1, G4, PC3, PC8, PC12, PC14, PC15, I4, R1, R3, R10, R11

Opera: A1, A2, A9, A11, G5, PC4

Ophthalmology: A3, R13

Oxford: PC1, PC6, PC17

Panoramas: A4

Pantheon: PC10

Paper (cost of): PC4

Parliament:

    --members listed: A9, PC4, R9

    --discussed by diarist: A2, A7, A10, PC6

Parliamentary Reform: A10

Passmore Edwards Settlement: I4

Penny Readings: G7

Pensions: PC4

Percival, Spencer (politician): A2, A3

Pilgrim's Progress: A7

Subject Index

Poe, Edgar Allan (American poet): PC12

Poetry:

    --printed in diary: A1, PC2, PC7

    --transcribed by diarist: A10, G4, PC11, PC17

Polhill, Frederick (M.P.): G3

Politics: A1, A2, A3, A4, A7, A8, A10, A12, G3, G5, I2, I3, R7, R8

Possessions (familial): I4, R5, R8

Post Office: A9, A10, G3, G7, PC18, I3

Poverty: A10, PC1, R8, R15

Powell, George Eyre (commander): R8, R10, R11

Primrose Societies: G7

Prince Albert:

    --death of: R9

    --wedding of: PC9

Prince Regent: See George IV

Princess Charlotte: PC4

Public Notaries: G3

Public Offices and Officers: A9, A10, G2, G3, PC4, PC13, I3

Punch Pocket-Book: PC13

Punctuation (incorrect use in diaries): A3, PC3, PC6, PC8

Quakers: R1

Queen Caroline: A1, A3

Queen Mab: PC14

Queen Victoria: A8, PC3, PC9, PC14

Racial Attitudes: R9

Radicalism: A3, A4

Railroads: G7, PC17, R6, R8

Ranching: A7, PC13, PC20

Reading (mentioned or listed): A1, A3, A7, A10, G1, G4, G6, PC2, PC6, PC11, PC12, PC14, PC15, PC20, I4, R2, R9, R10, R13

Readings (public): PC12, PC14, I3

Recipes: R14

Redundancy (of women): G4, PC15, PC20

Rouen Cathedral: A11

Royal Academy: A11

Royal Exchange: PC10

Royal Family (listed): A1, A9, G2, PC7, PC13, I3, R9

Sailing: G2

Sanitation: A4

Science: A3, I1, I2

Schiller, Friedrich von (German dramatist): A10

Scotland: G1, G5, PC14, R2, R7

Scott, Sir Walter (novelist): G5

Secretarial Duties: A4, G4, PC8, PC11, I1, I4

Self-Assessment: A1, A10, G4, PC2, PC4, PC8, PC19, I4, R1, R2, R3, R5, R6, R11, R15

Sermons: A1, A4, A10, A11, G4, PC3, PC8, PC14, I2, R6, R11

Servants: A5, A6, A8, A12, G3, PC5, PC11, PC12, I1, I2, I3, R3

Servants' Wages: A9, A12, PC4, PC7, PC18

Sexes, Relationship Between the: A10, G1, G6, PC8, PC10, PC11, PC13, PC14, PC19, R3, R10, R11, R13

Shakespeare, William (dramatist): A10

She Stoops to Conquer: A7

Shopping: A9, A13, PC10

Six Acts (1819): A3

Slang: R15

Slave Trade: R6

Smoking: PC15, R13

Sports: A3, A7, A12, G2, PC14, PC15, PC17, R9

Stephen, Sir Leslie (author): I4

Stockings (cost of): G7, PC4

Student's Journal: PC4

Sublimity: PC1, PC6

Suez Canal: A13

Suicide: R3

Sunday School: A3, R3, R8, R10

Superstition: G1

Sussex: R13

Surrey: PC14

Switzerland: A6, A11, G6, R15

Syntax:
    --complex: A1, A3, A8, A10, A13, PC1, PC5, PC8, PC14, PC20, R2, R3, R5, R6, R9, R13
    --fragmentary: A5, A6, A12, G3, G5, G7, PC3, PC4, PC11, PC13, I1, I2, I4, R11

Taxes: A9, A10, G3, PC4, PC13, I3

Teaching: A4, G3, G4, PC5, PC12, PC14, I4, R8, R10, R11

Telephone: I2

Tenants: R9

Tennyson, Lord Alfred (poet): A10, PC12

Thackeray, William Makepeace (novelist): PC12

Theater: A1, A4, A8, A11, A13, G3, G7, PC3, PC4, PC10, PC12, PC15, I3

Tintern Abbey: G6

Travel Journals: A1, A6, A11, G4, G6, PC2, PC6, PC10, PC17, PC20, I1, R1, R9, R13, R15

Typewriters: G7

<u>Uncle Tom's Cabin</u>: R10

Unitarianism: R8, R10, R11

University Terms (listed): A9, A10, A12, PC4, PC9, I3

<u>Unprotected, The</u>: I1

Vauxhall: A1, PC3

Verulam, Earl of: A2, A3

Vienna: I3

Visiting:

    --charitable: PC14, R1, R3, R6, R8, R10, R11

    --social: A1, A2, A5, A7, A8, A11, A13, G2, G3, PC3, PC4, PC6, PC12, PC14, PC15, I3, R5, R7, R12, R14

Wages (of day laborers): PC4

Wales: A8, G7, G8, PC1, PC6, PC16, PC18, R4, R10

Ward, Humphrey: I3

Waterloo: PC3

Weddings: A10, G6, PC3, PC6, PC12, R9, R10

Wellington, Arthur Wellesley, Duke of (statesman): PC2

Welsh: PC16

Wemyss, Francis (engineer): PC8

Westminster Bridge: PC6

Wet Nurse: PC3

Widowhood: A1, G1, PC15

Wilberforce, William (humanitarian): G4

William IV: A7, I1

Women:

--and social role: A7, A10, G6, PC8, PC13, PC15, PC19, I2, R10, R11

--English v. Australian: PC20

Woodeville, Elizabeth: R5

Worcestershire: PC17, R3

Wordsworth, William (poet): PC11

Writing (as liberation): PC19, I2

Wyatt, James (architect): PC1

Xenophobia: A1, A3, A13, R13

Yorkshire: R1